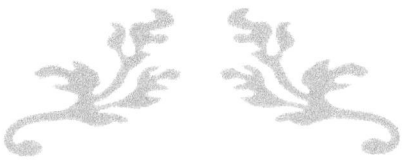

KALEIDOSCOPE

AN ANTHOLOGY OF POETRY

BY M HARLAND - SUDDES

WORKBOOK PRESS LLC
187 E Warm Springs Rd
Suite B285 Las Vegas NV 89119 USA

Website: https://workbookpress.com/
Hotline: 1-888-818-4856
Email: admin@workbookpress.com
Ordering Information:

Quantity sales. Special discounts are available on quantity purchases by corporations, associations, and others. For details, contact the publisher at the address above.

Library of Congress Control Number: 2024908492

ISBN-13: 978-1-963718-22-5 Paperback Version
          978-1-963718-23-2 Digital Version

REV. DATE: 06/17/2024

Dedication...

To: Oliver, Gaynor, Lindsay and William with much love, and appreciation for your encouragement and support.

Written Words…

Tangible evidence of MIND… and of our thoughts, and dreams, which still live on for a while, when we are gone into the great silence.

KALEIDOSCOPE

Life begins as a bright Kaleidoscope of ... *What might be...*

Filled with wild fantasies and dreams we hope to realise,

Exalting the mind, from our chaotic days of youth,

As we live those wild imaginings, in our dreams,

And romance life's pleasures, while *fancy* reigns supreme.

Until we discover, life's not a dream-machine where wishes flow...

And what we *think we need*, lives only in our heads...

The transient glow of youth fades with the years,

As the shadow-dust of time creeps slowly in.

We watch life's colours change, shaking up reality's fragments,

From sparkling rainbows into disillusioned grey.

Who can retain the flamboyant magic of youthful fantasies,

Against time's changing Kaleidoscope... where mocking mirrors blur,

Until only the certainty of the sun, and stars remain?

Nascentes morimur*

*each day we die a little

CONTENTS   PAGE

ASPECTS
OF
THE SEA

CORAL ISLAND FANTASY

(A spoken narrative with songs)

Prologue

So long ago, that memory fails to linger,

But in the days when silent ships blew far

Across the ocean from Earth's end to end,

A tale of oft repeated wonder

Told of a sea-witch, in the Southern seas…

Enchantress, who a fish's scales had taken,

And fashioned for herself a fin,

To so enshroud her legs, that she appeared

To be half woman, half ocean-dwelling fish.

Thus magic-laden, behold, a mermaid beauteous,

Her song when falling on men's ears,

Would drive all thoughts of safety from their minds,

And canvas sails would idle, as they hung in wonderment

From every beam and shroud, to hear.

Thus, many a ship was lured to its doom.

A faery isle can never be encompassed

Within the mundane plotting of a chart,

And so, survivors never could recall

Just where their doom had lingered on the sea.

Their memories recalled only vague images…

Visions of enchanted, underwater groves

Where coral grew like trees, and Neptune ruled…

And misty recollections of a faery song

Weaving a spell, which bound them into a world of dreams.

Calypso

Come where the mermaid waits,
Where her magic commands the air,
She calls, "Welcome… Aloha…Come!
Here is freedom for you to share

> Chorus… *Aloha! Aloha! Ah-nah, ah-nah, Aloha!*
> *Aloha! Aloha! Ah-nah, ah-nah, Aloha!*

Lay down the tools of work,
From all toil take your hands away,
Share the rhapsody of the deep
While in coral groves you sleep.

> Chorus…. *Aloha! Aloha! Ah-nah, ah-nah, Aloha! Etc.*

One day, young Jack, a Country Squire's son,

(A callow youth, close budding to a man...)

Encountered an ancient sailor, while wandering on the shore…

He… emblazoned with tattoos, and full of wondrous yarns…

Amazed and entranced the young lad's eager mind,

With stories of sea monsters, and creatures wild and free

That roamed the ocean depths… And of exotic distant lands…

Full of strange sights and sounds, to mystify and charm the eyes and ears;

And most captivating, to the young man's mind,

Was the tale of a bewitching mermaid… Neptune's Queen…

And of the magic spell she wove, which held him captive...

Long enchanted... deep in Neptune's Water-World…

And how he had at last escaped that curse, and come

Safe back to land-locked shores, after his long imprisonment.

And so, Jack whiled away that idle afternoon

Listening entranced, to those beguiling tales

Of adventures braved in far-off foreign seas,

And wondrous places he had never dreamt to see…

Then e'er they parted, and the lad made his adieu,

The withered mariner paused a moment, and from his knapsack

Drew forth an ocean relic… a conch… so wondrous bright

That sun, and moon, and stars dwelt on its rim…

"A fond remembrance," the grizzled sailor said,

"Of a time so long ago, my memories blur and fade."

Then laying his hand, in reverence, on his breast,

He said, "This wondrous shell, which I now give to you

Is all remaining to me of… THE MAID…

Take it, lad… I pray Good Fortune will attend your future voyaging,

And may your sorrows never greater be,

Because you now receive this mystic gift from me."

Jack took the offered shell incredulously…

"Good sir… you are too kind… I cannot take THIS… GIFT!

So strange and fair a treasure is worth a goodly sum…

Let me offer some recompense? Pray, take some reward from me?"

The answer came quickly, "This precious shell cannot be bought or sold,

Nor ever stolen… nor exchanged for jewels, or gold.

Its powerful, protective magic is an amulet, which must be… *given free…*

A benevolent gift… one offered between those who sail the seas.

My days before the mast, are past and gone,

Now I must keep, *to land*, until my life is done.

And so, I pass it happily now to thee.

I wish you contentment Jack, and safety on the ocean deeps,

And a quiet billet on land, before you take *your* final sleep."

Stanza 3

The lustrous, pearly shell-lights, entranced Jack's youthful mind,

And a hunger seemed to grow there. Suddenly

A thirst for adventure churned inside his thoughts…

"THE MAID! Could it be *she,* whose magic tale

Was told by old men around the winter fires?"

That mysterious enchantment captivated his heart and soul,

And an alien magic began to weave its secret spell…

"Why should I stay here, and waste my life growing old?

Harvesting fields, and tending sheep and cows?

I'll not squander my bright youth upon my father's land,

I'll compass the world… and explore its mysteries…

One month from now, MY MAJORITY, I'll gain!

Then I shall be a man… and **I vow… THIS MAN will go to sea!"**

"A SHIP! A SHIP!" he cried, "I'll sign aboard, and go
Where sandal-wooded island breezes blow…
And exotic perfumes richly scent the air!
A SHIP! A SHIP! I'll find this earthly paradise, and then,
From enchanted coral beaches I'll ne'er return again."

Jack's mind was fixed… his ambitions resolute and blind,
To seek adventures across salt waters wild,
And scour the Southern Ocean 'til he had found,
The enchanted island of, The Mermaid Queen…
Nor family, nor friends, could turn his mind, or change
His fixed resolve, to abandon his estates
And seek his fortune upon the perilous seas.

> ***Jack's Song…***
> *"Goodbye to England for ever,*
> *Something is calling me on,*
> *To seek a future far from here*
> *And I'm eager to be gone.*
> *Spice islands somewhere lie waiting*
> *Their magic is working on me,*
> *And perfumes from another world*

Weave enchantments I long to see…

I'll search the days and the starlight,

On foam my pathway will toss,

Till far away in the tropic skies

Brightly shines, The Southern Cross.

Farewell to my old home forever,

An enchantment is calling me on

To seek my future far from here

And I'm eager to be gone."

Stanza 4

A golden dawn came stealing to the sky…

Contented hammocks swung beneath the decks,

And warmly a gentle breeze stirred up the scented air,

While gently, the heaving sails the vessel bore

Silently, on its course, across the tranquil sea.

But that fair dawn brought not well-omened day…

A ripple of faint harmony, insinuated the morning breeze,

And snatches of soft voices bewitched the languid air,

While vague, capricious taunting seemed to float

Upon the water, stirring up the cresting waves.

And all around, an enchantment meandered through that early dawn,

Exciting the lapping waves, until it seemed

It was the music bore the vessel on its way.

It breathed its strange magic, and swelled the flaccid sails,

And caressed the sailors' drowsy ears, until they woke…

Then clamouring to the deck, the mariners came.

> "What harmony of song-birds do we hear?
>
> "What music comes to charm the night away?
>
> "What choir of angels speaks to us of Heaven?"

Captivated and charmed, the hearty crew

Suddenly fell deeply enervated… confused, bemused, entranced…

When that strange enchantment o'er powered their minds.

And all the yards, and sheets, and steering gear

Lay slack, and untended, on that doomed barque…

Then…of a sudden, an unearthly vision came,

Rising majestically from beneath the azure waves…

And thus, The Mermaid, rose… She a glowing, jewelled star,

Glittering enchantress, mistress of old Neptune's fabled world…

To hear her song, a hundred men stood dumb…

Time hung suspended, as Jack gazed, transfixed,

While glowing in the sunlight, glowed THE MAID…

And to his addled mind it seemed she called to him…

For his bewildered senses clearly heard her say…

"Welcome! Aloha! Come… Peace and Freedom lie here with me,

In Neptune's glorious coral groves, beneath this tranquil sea."

In that bewitching moment his heart was lost,

For no earthly maid that Jack had ever seen,

For beauty and radiance, could match old Neptune's queen.

She crooned to him softly, and beckoned him to come…

Cast off all thoughts of labour, care, and strife,

For she could offer him much more enchantment,

Than ever, could be found within his earthly life…

No pain or anguish would ever more, touch his brow…

The kingdom of Neptune, promised him… **Paradise**… NOW!

Calypso

    Come where the mermaid waits,

    Hear her magic command the air

    She calls, "Welcome! Aloha! Come…

    Here is freedom for you to share.

    chorus… Aloha! Aloha! Ah-nah, ah-nah, Aloha!

Aloha! Aloha! Ah nah, ah nah, Aloha!

Lay down the tools of work,
From all toil take your hands away,
Share the rhapsody of the deep,
Peace and freedom lie just this way.

chorus... Aloha! Aloha! Ah-nah, ah-nah, Aloha! etc

Stanza 5

And while that haunting, faery music, entranced
And confused the weary sailors' uncomprehending minds,
The good ship floundered, and wallowed on the sea...
Until suddenly... like a bolt from thunder clouds... CRASH!
Hidden, jagged rocks had sundered the hull,
And cleft its sturdy oaken beams.
Ravaged and broken, the vessel lurched and groaned,
As it was driven, remorselessly upon rocks beneath her keel,
Its timbers shuddered, in death-throes anguished moans.
Then a thousand devilish fathoms tore at her wounded sides...
And mountainous, serpent waves, found entrance given.
At starboard and larboard... they rendered her, stem to stern...
Foundering her quickly, and sinking her below...

While the morning sun continued shining… silently watching her go!

Mariners were flung to ravening sharks,

Encircling the tragic vessel's shattered hull…

Strong men no effort made to save themselves,

When trapped in powerful magic they fell supine…

Their valiant-bodies, muscles and sinews, useless to the last!

That day a hundred men sank helpless, to their doom!

Dreaming it seemed… not drowning, upon that evil morn…

Gracefully sinking down through the azure waves…

Eye-to-eye with unblinking, curious fish…

Jack dumbly wondered as he slowly sank below,

Whether he was soaring skywards? Or plunging to depths below?

All reality had deserted him, and his senses could not tell,

If he was bound for Heaven… Or entering some devilish Hell.

Silence befriended him… He grasped his enchanted shell…

Clinging to it reassured him, that all might yet be well.

Bright colours gleamed everywhere; and when his feet touched sand,

It seemed on powdered silver clouds he trod…

Scattered around him lay great coffers, gaping wide,

Each over-flowing with seductive treasures,

Long since abandoned, beneath that treacherous island's tide.

Then mysteriously, a pulsating warning came from within the shell…

And a voice in his head spoke more clearly than any clarion bell…

"Beware young sailor… Steady as you go!

For a greater, more perilous danger now approaches you,

Down here below!"

Stanza 6

That fabled… Coral Island… was no heavenly paradise,

But an evil, treacherous den, where malevolent harpies bide.

A place where bewitching decoys lured brave men to their graves,

To satisfy a mermaid queen,

And fill, with treasure, King Neptune's coral caves…

Jack saw entombed within that royal treasury…

A charnel-house… a grave-yard… nothing more…

Where the lifeless bodies of the comrades he had known,

Now lay abandoned… wrecked flotsam, adrift upon a cruel tide…

And he wept at what he saw, so savagely revealed, on every side…

Scattered among seductive treasures, all tumbled far and wide,

Lay the rotting hulks of fine vessels, now stripped of their maritime pride.

This was a desolate boneyard, where fishes and octopus played,

And where no merry hornpipe was ever danced... nor any anchor -rope belayed.

Death and destruction faced Jack there below,

Among those forests of swaying kelp, in lagoons where bright corals grow.

While around him the treasures of the Earth, spilled forth their untold wealth,

Garishly lighting that tragic scene... and its mockery of human death.

Suddenly, there came the rumble of heavy, approaching wheels,

And an enormous, gilded war-chariot quickly became revealed,

It bore the monstrous presence, of the cruel Ocean King...

And from some secret, hidden place, a fearsome voice boomed loud,

It fell upon Jack's ears, commanding, powerful and proud.

Jack trembled in terror, and tighter clutched his talisman shell,

And he dropped upon his knees, quaking from fear,

While the ominous war-chariot, and its master, now drew near.

Stanza 7

"BOY! Give to me that conch shell, I see now in your hand…

It is an ocean jewel… not something paltry, from the land!

I DEMAND, upon this instant, that it be returned to ME…

Restored to its rightful owner… The GOD-KING of the SEA!

You need fear nothing… It is of little worth for you to lose,

And I will reward you richly… You may take what e'er you choose.

Come! Look around… you may rifle my treasure chests…

Take what you will… You may select the best.

JUST RETURN TO ME that conch… For you it holds no worth…

Though for me it is more highly prized, than all these jewels of Earth…

I SAY AGAIN… Give back my precious ocean shell!

Or I swear I will see you rot, in my darkest, deepest hell…"

For an instant Jack glimpsed the cruelty glittering in Neptune's eyes,

And he recognised the cunning treachery there, to steal away his prize…

Here lay no mercy, nor any generous thought…

As in that Ocean's domains, he humbly knelt, before its tyrant Lord.

Surrender the shell? It was the precious, mysterious charm,

Which had safely protected him, against the deep seas' harm…

While all his shipmates lay drowned and scattered wide,

The conch had cast its magical, life-saving spell

About him, and kept him safe from Neptune's deadly hell…

And while he held it securely within his grasp,

The fury of the ocean-world could never destroy him, ever…

Whatever demonic wickedness Neptune might conjure, or endeavour."

"The shell is mine," Jack said, "I will not let it go,

And all the jewels of Earth, are useless here below…

The sea is cruel… and you are man's treacherous enemy,

I'll keep MY shell… Your baubles will bring no joy…

There's no compassion, here beneath your savage waves,

Only sunken ships, and poor dead sailors' graves…

But I will not fear the typhoon's raging swell…

When in my hands I hold my talisman shell."

Stanza 8

The sea-king's towering fury, instantly became a fearsome sight…

He raged and stormed, and curdled the day into night.

"Then, foolish mortal, I condemn you to a living death, below…

For never more, will you from my kingdom go…

Upon you now, I place my curse… that you,

AND THE CONCH, will stay,

Trapped here in my domain, for ever and a day…

For this displeasure, you will ne'er escape from me,

Nor ever end your living-death, here beneath the sea…

My prisoner you will remain… THE guardian of MY PRECIOUS SHELL,"

He roared a hideous laugh. "And here you will remain,

Until some ocean devil comes to release you from my powerful, binding chain."

Peals of hollow laughter echoed inside Jack's head…

As the vengeful sea-king hissed, "You'll soon wish that you were dead."

Within an instant he had summoned up a great typhoon…

And the heavens above turned black, as the sun fought with the moon.

Lightning forked into the water… mountainous waves bore down,

Lifting and tumbling Jack, within the fury of that storm,

And submerging him in surging fathoms of, raging, deadly foam.

Beneath the waves the seabed heaved with Neptune's ire,

Dragging and pummelling Jack, to reclaim that one desire…

But nothing tore away Jack's talisman shell…

It remained, his staunch defence, against that deadly hell.

Then battered and choking, gasping for air and breath,

Jack felt himself wrestling with Neptune's deadly, sea-demons of death.

At length, the vengeful storm threw him into a quiet cave…

A rocky, submarine refuge against the sea-king's rage.

And as he lingered, clinging faintly to the edge of life,

Broken, wounded, and abandoned, in that savage strife,

And drifting in mind... it seemed his own death knell

Reached out to him, with the sonorous chiming of a bell.

Now, his salt-blind eyes stared wildly towards the coral trees,

As a regal procession approached him, through the now calm, and limpid seas…

And from a radiant portal, studded with bright jewels

A mermaid band led forth a cavalcade

Of silver seahorses, tossing their silken manes…

All richly garlanded with exotic sea-blooms…

Anemones, alive and glowing, in colours like rainbow flames…

Thus, smiling beguilingly, and calling him by name,

King Neptune's Consort… the fair Miranda came.

Her words were gentle, and fell softly on Jack's ears,

As in his wretched state, she spoke to calm his fears.

"Sailor, I vow that no further harm will blight your future days,

If you will now accept, and wear, this enchanted pearly lei…

Take it Jack, for in tranquil safety I seek to protect your stay.

These pearls will guard you in the sea-king's realm,

And while you wear them, sleep will quieten your troubled mind...

Here you must remain; but my magic lei will protect your life,

And be your safety barrier, against King Neptune's strife."

Then around Jack's neck a garland of great and lustrous pearls

The mermaid band so carefully laid on…

And in an instant every fearful thought

Faded and fell away, and Jack's eyes drooped,

As into peaceful slumber he slipped content.

Mermaids' song*... Golden sunshine, silver waves*

Endless jewelled coral caves,

Here we stay and free from care

Winding ribbons in our hair.

Goodbye sorrow, goodbye care

Winding ribbons in our hair. (repeat)

You will never more awake
Now these magic pearls you take,
Peace will always crown your brow
As you drift in slumber now…

Goodbye sorrow, goodbye care
Winding ribbons in our hair. (repeat)

Stanza 9

Never a wave, never a tropic storm

Ruffled his quiet dreams… and so Jack stayed…

If he had ever dwelt outside those coral caves

All was forgotten, in his enchanted sleep.

Miranda's beauteous face, and shining sapphire eyes

Had drained all fear of danger, leaving only contentment there…

But securely clasped in his hands lay the glittering shell…

Miranda smiled, and touched a silver bell…

Swirling in dreams a fantasy on Jack she laid…

He smiled contentedly in sleep… but never stirred.

His life in coral-dream-world had begun,

Now he was content to dream, and never waken to the sun.

Mermaids' song... *Close your eyes in happy sleep*

Feel the rhythm of the deep.

Listen to the song we sing

And th' enchantment that we bring.

Goodbye sorrow, goodbye care

Winding ribbons in our hair. (repeat)

And so, the enchanted months and years slipped by…

While Jack dreamed, in the grotto of Old Neptune's queen.

His beard grew long… but strange to tell… not hair

But seaweed, green and tenuous, straggled around him there

Like a cloak. Among its tangle, fishes played,

And passing oysters stopped to admire those pearls

Of wondrous beauty, hanging around his neck.

Their magic lustre never grew the less...

But where they had come from… none of them could guess.

Magic never owns any conscience, rhyme, or reason…

And mermaids are capricious, and as changeable as the season…

Those fickle-hearted witches ever sought for new, amusing toys…

And Miranda soon forgot about her enchanted sailor boy…

So… Jack was left to dream the passing years away,

Bewitched, and quite forgotten, in that coral grotto where he lay,

Stanza 10

Mischief can take on many different shapes…

A cloud… a playful breeze… an ocean Jackanapes…

And unexpectedly, one day… at last a… *mischief* came…

Investigating… curious… cautiously looking round…

Bright eyes peeping out… Seeming to ask the question…

"WHO IS HERE ABOUT? …

"WHAT'S THIS?

Naughty mermaids stealing oysters' pearls,

And weaving wicked spells… Causing poor crabs,

And lobsters, untold harms, with their most wicked

And tormenting, cruel, and hurtful charms?

I'm a CRAB! Snip-snap! I hunt among the weeds"…

DING DONG! "What's that I heard?… A warning bell?

I'm doing no harm… Snip Snap!

Just innocently slashing weeds from rocks and shells…

TAKE CARE! Mermaids may be returning now?… Snip-snap!

There's none can tell what fiendish plans

Can come about from their small hands…

Or what their devious minds can plan…

Opening shells of giant clam…

Laying traps for unwary eels…

And shameful teasing of baby seals… Snip-snip! Snip-snap!"

Song of the Crab…

"There's a slapping and cracking

Of seaweed that's wrapping the rocks.

And a scratching and scraping of barnacles

Down at the docks.

I can hide in the sand,

Crawl about upon land,

Stare an octopus straight in the eye.!

These tough nippers of mine

Can cut through thickest twine…

As down in the fathoms I lie.

They're amazing and strange,

All the stories that I have to tell…

I'm a gypsy who travels the world,

And my home is a shell…

There's no place I've not been,

Not a sight still unseen,

From the China to Indian seas…

But I like to keep cooool

In a green seashore pooool…

And I do as I jolly-well please!

What a life… wild and free…

Sink or swim… it's for ME!

I'm a snippety, snappety, crotchety, cratchety…

Rusty old… crusty old… CRAB!"

"WHAT'S THIS?" The crab paused to take a prod at Jack.

"It's a MAN! Not dead, I think…

Enchanted by the look of him… snip! snap!

Another of those wicked mermaids' spells…

And fashioned to keep this poor sailor in their cruel, bedevilled hell!

Gadzooks! Garlanding him with enchanted, stolen pearls, is clever,

To keep him from the human world… for ever…

But there's no time for me to linger longer…

It's time for me to go… and find a safe crevice,

Somewhere down below… Before the sea-maids catch me here!

BUT... STOP!!!

Let me pause to consider this golden opportunity... MMMMM!

Revenge seems sweeter, when achieved by means of accidental NORMALITY!

I see no reason, here beneath the sea, to inflict unnecessary pain, or brutality...

MY simple REVENGE, requires only the SLIP of one accidental claw...

Then , one brief moment to savour my satisfaction... and OFF I SHALL GO... NOTHING MORE!

Leaving you, poor sailor, liberated, and forever FREE,

From Neptune's painful coral halls, deep beneath the sea...

HAHA! Snip Snap!

For MY sweet REVENGE... no one will ever guess, WHY, or ever know, WHO?"

"YES! One final *snip*, before I go… HA-HA!

I'll leave my own brand of torment, for that mermaid band, here below.

SNIP! SNAP!"

Suddenly, only the echoing voice of the vengeful crab remained...

"I'm a snippety, snappety, crotchety, cratchety,

Rusty old, crusty old... crab"...

Then, in *one brief, fateful moment... SUDDENLY…*

SLASH!

Cascading pearls came tumbling far and wide...

Bouncing, and bubbling... dancing wide... carefree...

"The spell is broken... NOW! Sailor man... you are FREE!"

Only a pair of crab's gleaming eyes peeped out briefly from a rocky ledge,

Then disappeared rapidly, having kept his resolute pledge.

Stanza 11

Strange misty shapes bemused Jack's clouded eyes,

As up through the salty water, he suddenly felt propelled...

Clasping his pearly shell, in his pale and withered hands...

He briefly glimpsed a richly jewelled hall...

And lustrous golden weed... Or was it, mermaid hair?

And a beauteous princess seated in a Royal chair...

Then choking, and half drowned, his old lungs fought for air.

At length, the sea coughed up its human toy,

Flung him towards the surface, confused and stunned.

While visions passed him by, as up he lunged...

Snatches of mermaid songs, reached his waterlogged, buzzing ears,

And half-calmed, and half-bemused, his long-forgotten fears.

A gentle wave at last, onto a sun-kissed shore

Brought Jack, and laid him softly on the quiet sand…

An aged mariner now… marooned and far from home…

It seemed that far away, deep in the ocean's swell

Old Jack could hear the mournful echo of a parting bell.

Songs of enchantment had filled his head, for many days,

While he had lain asleep, deep in those coral caves.

And now his senses he could no longer trust…

At last, his eyes were open… and his wild hands thrust,

To grasp the fading vision, which he sees no more…

Then saltier than the sea, flowed a river of bitter tears…

No coral caverns… no beauteous mermaids' song…

Just sand and sea… and sea… and sand and sky…

And his gleaming, pearly shell, which lay twinkling nearby.

So often we are torn between desire

For that which, IS… and what we most ASPIRE.

Mermaids' parting song

Ended is our magic spell

Sailor, we bid you farewell…

You may never more return

To our coral, ocean home…

Broken pearls are scattered near,

We may no-more keep you here,

From enchanted sleep below

And our singing, you must go.

Golden sunshine, silver waves

Endless jewelled coral caves,

Here we stay, and free from care,

Winding ribbons in our hair.

   Repeat; Here we stay and free from care

    Winding ribbons in our hair.

Stanza 12

The ship which bore Jack safely, far away,

Billowed and tossed the seas, full many a day.

He constantly scanned the ocean, with tired and aching eyes,

But only dolphins, and mewing seagulls there he spied.

His memories, were ever working, on that half-forgotten dream,

Of a fair face, elusive… the face of a queen…

And songs sung by mermaids, with eyes blue or green…

Only one souvenir was not lost to the deep,

His shell of enchantment, which had guarded his sleep.

And the sun, moon, and stars, ever danced on its rim…

A conch, faceless… but magic, and ever precious to him.

Jack's song

Trade winds are blowing
To carry me home...
Smiling eyes I see,
Goodbye... Adieu... Aloha... Now
Where will my home be?
If I had fate in my pocket,
Bottled magic in store,
I'd empty all the ocean wide
To find what I'm searching for...
Ocean is wide and empty now,
Coral caves are gone,
A wand'rer now till time shall end,
Always I must roam...
Trade winds are blowing
To carry me home
Smiling eyes I see,
Goodbye... Adieu... Aloha... NOW...
Where will my home be?

CROSSING THE BAR

Look, where the passing of the evening light
Pauses in splendour, gilding the lonely sea.
I thank my maker for such pure delight
Made by that lingering, westward falling star.
This night, of all the nights I've ever lived,
I'd will, such joy and beauty to endure.
But I know I must leave when day has fled.
The tide that bears me hence is on the turn,
The compass set, my course marked in the stars.
And I must journey onward into night,
Trailing in wake of comrades gone ahead,
This fair horizon, fading from my sight.
Somewhere I hear a sea-gull's plaintive cry
Urging me to make ready for floodtide…
Fine-trim the rigging, weigh anchor and be gone!
Soft, swirling sea-fret steals upon my mind
And weariness overwhelms my aching heart…
Dark clouds draw closer round me from the hills,
And sirens' songs steal softly on my ears,
Lulling my drowsy senses with desire.
In such enchanted dreaming let me sleep,

Deep, peaceful longing, heavy on my eyes…

I mark the helmsman, half concealed in mist,

And know him for the pilot of my soul…

I've seen him in the shadows many-a-time,

But never have I felt him close before.

Lead onward, helmsman, guide this sailor home…

My destination lies where soft waves break,

Beyond the shoals and reefs of grief and tears,

To freedom in lagoons, where trade-winds sleep…

Now, shadows darken on the grey sea's face,

And you and I will cross the bar tonight,

THE SONG OF THE SEA

Seagulls are calling! The ocean's my road,

Wide and wild and free.

Music like rolling thunder is filling my ears,

Singing, "Sailor come forth with me!"

My heart beats to the rhythm of that anthem,

And it burns in my mind like a fire,

While the raging surf, and the billowing sky,

Feed this torment of desire.

I'm in thrall to a heartless mistress,

Who has stolen my reason away,

She has lashed my soul to the kicking wheel,

As she drives me on my way.

Her, *Song of The Sea,* holds me spellbound,

And it offers me no hope of release,

While her distant horizons beckon,

Though my weary heart longs for peace.

Unknown dangers may challenge my sinews,

With what may yet lie in wait,

'Neath the stormy skies, and the towering waves,

Where I go to confront my fate.

Through daylight, and starlight I must wander,

Wherever my vessel may toss,

Till half a world away in the tropic skies,

Brightly shines, *The Southern Cross*.

I dream of distant islands,

And a place where at last I may rest,

When, *The Song of The Sea*, grows silent,

And I have finished my quest.

But that lies somewhere in the future,

In a place I may never reach,

For the Earth turns, and the sun burns,

And the heavens have much to teach.

At grey dawn the tide will be turning,

The wind will blow southward and strong,

Swelling the sails, when the anchor's weighed,

And urging me to be gone…

Seagulls are calling! The ocean's my road,

Wide and wild and free,

Music like rolling thunder is filling my ears,

Singing, "Sailor, come forth with me!"

A NORTHUMBRIAN MEMORY

Beyond the rugged walls of Bamburgh's towers,

Where marram-clothed dunes defy the sea,

I watched the fishing boats returning home.

They seemed to hover on the tired tide

Like sea birds heavy laden from a meal.

With engines cut, they cruised towards the shore,

The oily water heaving 'gainst their keels.

That evening sky was filled with screaming gulls

Wheeling a raucous welcome to the catch,

Scenting the dead fish heaped down in the hold,

And snatching what offal might be hurled their way.

The fading daylight yawned across the sea

Far out, where the Longstone Light, had guided their homeward way.

And as the quiet vessels nosed their leeward tack,

The weary crews in oilskins, waited by the rails,

Their sand-encrusted creels, and nets, already stowed…

Their salt-stung eyes, and thoughts, all fixed on home…

Then past the solemn red-eye, blinking on the pier,

They glided into the harbour's waiting arms,

Enduring their final bird-embattled lap,

With masts thrusting like spears, against the darkening sky.

ASPECTS

OF

WAR

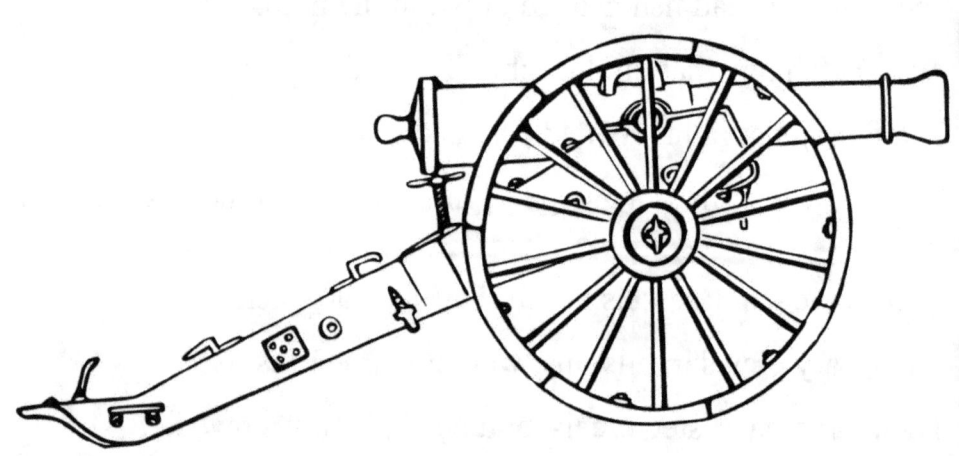

RETURN TO SEPTEMBER 1940

(Reminiscences of A Battle-of- Britain veteran)

"I cannot escape my dreams, they will not let me be,

They lurk where memories flourish in my brain,

Transmuting into chaos while I sleep…

Those ghosts from the past creep in, to haunt my nights,

And carry me back to days when I was young.

I find myself racing along the dunes

In summer shorts, my brown legs bounding on

Barefoot, with wind-blown hair across my eyes,

Frantic to launch my kite towards the sun,

Screeching ten years of pent-up childish glee.

Then, in the next instant, my head is filled with din,

Persistent blaring from the klaxon horn,

Screaming its alert… its call to arms…

"Enemy aircraft approaching from the South…"

Deafened by battle noise, my nerves are primed to fight…

My feet weighed down by heavy flying boots…

I grab my kit, and head out for the field...

Racing across the runway, to my "SPIT".

Scrambling to get aloft, and gain some height...

Five minutes before the Stukas rain down hell!

Five minutes, from devastation from above!

But in those minutes, I know I'll hit the clouds...

These are the replayed hauntings in my head...

The memories infesting the chambers of my sub-consciousness.

Imprinted in a never-ending loop.

Conditioned memories, of where my duty lay,

Reminding me, PER ARDUA AD ASTRA...

My fate was written daily, in the stars.

Suddenly... I rouse in confusion, feeling out-of-place...

Thrashing around, wild-eyed, to get a grip

On what reality I currently occupy...

Still clinging to life... One left of those who flew...

A relic of long-past days... One of, "The-Few".

What did we know of, *WAR*, who scarce had lived?

We'd read the history of our nation's past,

Of blood-soaked battle fields, and great heroic deeds...

Then Destiny rolled the fatal dice again,

Proclaiming a new and brutal war afoot…

With all of Europe fallen, our island stood alone…

And we were called, to hold the vital line…

Bring our youth and vigour to that bloody game,

And turn the tide that threatened dire defeat.

So, *play we must*, or be-forever-damned…

We fought because it was our country's need.

We bit-the-bullet, took up the gauntlet thrown,

We were no lily-livered cowards holding back,

Appeasing the enemy, and his *crooked cross*…

Or nervous of what might come before day's end…

We grasped each moment and squeezed life's juice from it.

Our call to arms, the siren's dismal wail…

The senseless wreckage, and the death strewn all around…

Win… or be beaten? It doesn't leave much choice.

Those times are etched like acid in my brain.

But never did I feel so keenly… *live…*

As when, squeezed in the cockpit of my kite,

My fingers stuttered out a hail of shells

That brought the sky alive, with falling fire…

VAE VICTIS... Woe to the vanquished!

"Go, Merlin-GO! Climb from the stricken field,

And throw me up to where the danger lies!"

Hurricane and Spitfire, hurtling to attack...

Where only... The Best... were worthy of acclaim,

Counting in fives, the tally of their *kill*!

We'd point our nosecones skyward, climb like hawks,

Higher and ever higher, widening the gap,

Gaining the advantage only height could give.

Circling the heavens.... Not eagles seeking prey,

But deadly angels, flying on metal wings.

Fingers on triggers, eyes focused, minds alert,

Patrolling and scanning each quadrant of the sky....

Seeking to intercept the enemy, bring him down...

Peering with long-eyes, hard into the glare,

Anticipating the deadly quarry coming North...

With pulsating adrenalin throbbing in the brain,

Excitement smothering every latent fear,

And war-drums pounding with the propeller's beat.

That's how we survived those fateful, weary days.

Gladiators... arena masters... armed to fight and win,

Craving no quarter… nor ever quarter giving.

Air battles are best fought by young, foolhardy men

Inspired by invincibility's thick shield,

Lads who'd… swing on the devil's tail, and never baulk…

With needle precision calculating every swerve and dive,

Machine and pilot, fused into one power.

And… WHAT of Death? Push that grim thought aside,

Such brooding is best left to dry old men,

Whose thin blood creeps with caution through their veins.

We boiled with energy, patriotism, pride,

And that wild recklessness known only by the young.

Like lions we charged the runway, nostrils flared,

Scenting the quarry… racing for the kill!

"To sweep the Nazis hoards from out our skies!"

That was the mission. "Send them down to Hell!"

Our enemy seemed NOT made of flesh and bone…

We played our deadly game against, *machines.*

Our aerial hide-and-seek among the clouds

Was battling against dark emissaries of Hell.

We felt no glory where the contrails scarred the sky,

But damned-bad-luck, on friends who were shot down.

Refuel, rearm, fly, fight, land… start again…

That was the measure of those endless days,

With diving, whining Stukas screaming through the skies,

And Messerschmitts, and Heinkels, manoeuvring on our tails.

We held that aerial battle every day,

While death came droning out of every cloud.

But when each frantic, murderous op. was done,

And what was left of, "Adolph's" crew, limped south,

We'd gather, in the mess, to let off steam,

Argue our share of "kills", recount each strike.

Laugh heartily, brag who did what, and how…

Smoke a few fags, and tell some whopping tales,

Down a few beers, then crash to senseless sleep…

Too numb to wonder, "What time will they be back?"

The dying; wounded; mutilated, burnt,

Seemed vaguely in a parallel universe…

A place where wounds were treated, *all made well*…

And those who'd, "bought it…" went to some-place else.

Their names all listed as, "The Glorious Dead."

Though what was, *glorious,* being on that list,

Or being dead, and lost to happier times,

Utterly failed to inspire our venial goals.

Their empty seats were taken… squadron gaps closed-up,

Fresh crew, and planes delivered factory new…

And we lived on, to fight another day.

We gulped our grief, drank deep to dear friends lost,

Mourned them… prayed for them, and shed a tear…

Then got back to the job of hunting "Fritz."

Tomorrow? Well, that was a day unborn.

Our time was, NOW, to live it to the full.

We were too young to brood on… *what-might-be.*

How long we'd live… or how the end might come.

We were at war… a beast demanding blood!

The Boche had started it… so let them take the flack!

We'd bloodied their noses… and let them swim for France.

They called us, HEROES! Whatever heroes are?

But glory seldom figured in our plan.

We diced with danger, faced it every day,

Strafed, and were strafed, by blazing cannon fire.

It was the way we toiled all summer long

While we were fresh-faced boys straight out of school.

Our lives were distilled, like perfume, under fire,

Morphing us from youths to fighting men.

We learned survival skills the hardest way,

Not sitting softly in some chalk-filled room…

But facing our deadly enemy, gun for gun!

We tasted life's wine… and drank our fill of it…

The sour, the sweet, the vintage… and the dregs!

Age creeps upon you, like a dose of flu

That hangs around, and pills and booze won't cure,

Slowly sucking your vital force away,

And changing you into someone you don't know.

It steals away your acuity of thought,

While joints and muscles stiffen and grow frail.

Age creases your face, and leaves you trembling hands,

And eyes that can't see clearly anymore.

But deep within that secret, hidden place

Inside the head, past martial exploits play,

Interposing, when you close your eyes in sleep…

To call alive those long-past, glory days…

Aging has been a boring, downhill slide,

A tragic anti-climax, to all that went before…

Filled with a different sort of, "Battling-on,"
"Sticking-it-out," and, "Waiting-for-the-end."

Some memories, like scars, last all life through,
And there are good ones mixed among the bad.
I've come to terms with much of what has passed,
And I still don't worry what tomorrow holds…

For now… I'll take my chances… Till I'm grounded…
With luck… perhaps, I'll wake among the stars!"

"Per Ardua Ad Astra". In memory of all the British and allied airmen, who fought to preserve the freedom of Great Britain, against the Nazis, in "The Battle of Britain", Summer 1940.

THE MAPLE TREES AT VIMY RIDGE

(The Canadian War memorial at: Vimy Ridge: WW1)

"We came in Freedom's cause… With hopes and dreams,

And valiantly fought and died… Were sacrificed…

Scythed by machine-gun fire, and blown apart…

Hung out on wire in no-man's-land; and gassed

In rat-runs, fit for vermin, lice, and worms.

It was our destiny, to die and be forgot.

No more for us the Rocky Mountains of our native land,

The rolling wheat-fields, and white rivers log-jammed floes.

We lie beneath the battle-weary fields, and alien soil

Of Passchendaele and Ypres, in nameless graves.

The courage, and the fear, we wrote in blood and carved in bone,

All faded into lines in history books.

And so, our destiny of sorrow was fulfilled.

As silent witness' to our sacrifice and pain,

The noble maples have endured the years.

Each Fall, their gold and red, thick-paves the road we trod

Into forgotten holes, and fractured tombs.

We are the timeless youth who never aged!

We are the lost, the unfulfilled… the dead!

Sound *The Last Post*, at Menin's sombre Gate!

The bugle will not call one lost day back.

Our hopeful tomorrows lie at VIMY RIDGE,

With rusted bayonets, and long-forgotten dreams.

Yet still, our guard of honour keeps its watch,

With roots dug deep, in earth we made our own,

Sweet with the blood we shed. THEY do not sleep.

Each year, the maples bleed for us… and clothe our cenotaph…

They are our testament… our hope of life to come."

THE DE-BRIEFING

"It's time to make our move!" The captain said.

"Silence and speed are what we need tonight…

Surprise, makes all the difference to success…

So lads, we can't risk helicopters, going in…"

Someone muttered, "And what of our return?

"Will there be air support, to get us out?"

The reply came slowly… with a shaken head,

And a half-smile, which never reached his eyes…

"We won't know that… until the job's been done…

Or how many of us will need to be retrieved…

Let's cross those bridges when we get to them."

We trudged like yetis from the base that night,

Black faced, with shining eyes like glowing coals…

Just silent shadows bound for no-man's land…

A stealthy file, three paces twixt each man,

As into the shadowy valley, we moved away…

Prowling along the river's midnight shade,

With automatic weapons cradled across our chests…

Our fingers poised on triggers… anticipating the worst…

And bandoliers of grenades secured around our hips…

Stealthily we moved towards the secret rendezvous…

No jokes, no whispered oaths, that moon-free night…

We held the rule of silence… sacred… to a man…

Of what befell in that dark, alien place,

No accurate written record ever will be made…

But when it was too late for turning back,

Or taking cover among the quiet rocks…

They turned machine guns on us where we stood,

And made of that river valley a bloody swamp…

We'd been expected… Some infiltrator had betrayed the op.

But to a man we stood our ground and fought…

Yes… every soldier there, kept… *Duty's Pledge*…

And bloodied, but unbowed, each hero stood…

With automatics and grenades, we fought them back,

And what a hellish blaze we made that night…

'Til none of the enemy crew remained alive…

And we were left with every bullet spent,

Surrounded by the shattered remnants of our heroism…

Some softly called their mother's name…

Some slipped into the darkness with a sigh…

But it was silence and darkness that had led us there…

And silence and darkness now brought us back again…

Fewer in number… but with… Mission Fulfilled…

And the deafening noise of battle in between…

And those of us who lived… limped wounded, back to base,

To fight again… and find a different grave.

NIL DESPERANDUM

On this night of fear and sorrow I drown in a merciless sea,

Of overwhelming dangers which endeavour to encompass me.

In these hours of desolate darkness, where shall I find a friend?

Or someone who will grasp my hand… and strength and courage lend?

Dark conflicts overwhelm me, which I cannot hope to fight,

And I am wandering blindly, devoid of all hope or light…

Then into my tormented confusion, come silent angelic wings,

And a still, small voice of comfort, which an unseen presence brings…

"Take courage, for there is always one, who will never cast you aside…

"One who never fails to listen, and walks always by your side…

"Even to the bleakest darkness, God always returns the light…

"Hold to your faith… take courage, as you face and endure this fight!"

"BEGONE DESPAIR!" I answer, "I will stand firm 'gainst this mortal foe…

"And keep faith with my Eternal Friend, and the help He alone, can bestow."

THE SONG OF VINDOLANDA

The spirit of Vindolanda, still breathes her old song,

And she weaves her rich tapestry, of days lost and gone.

When... the Stanegate was trod, by the armies of Rome,

Then the Castra, which housed them, lay far from their home.

From Pons Aelius to the Solway, stands old, 'Hadrian's Wall,'

Where the mile-castle sentries, guarded what might befall...

Now the legions are vanished, from beneath Cheviot skies,

But, beneath, 'The Old Wall,' Vindolanda still lies.

In my mind gleams the sparkle of cold, frosty dawns,

And the crisp snows of winter, still whiten her lawns;

There... bright summer... still dances, in each moorland burn,

And the lost ghosts of Vindolanda, still dream of return.

I hear bagpipes skirling, down the shadows of time,

Where Rome's legions once gathered... and still, flows The
Tyne.

There the cavalry galloped, beneath the 'Old Wall,'

To the echoes of trumpets, before the nightfall.

The song of Vindolanda, tells of days that are fled...

And the legions which fought there, are centuries dead.

Yet still stands 'The Old Wall'... defiant and proud,

Where sleeping Vindolanda stirs, beneath her fair shroud.

The song of Vindolanda, is sleeping, not gone...

And the Legions still linger, for their footprints are strong...

And their landmarks in History are stamped far and wide,

While the 'Old Wall,' and Vindolanda[1], still bravely abide.

---

[1] Vindolanda AD 85- 370 (White Lawns). Important ROMAN Military Garrison, established during earliest Phase of Roman Britain's northern frontier, with access to Stanegate route, east to west and coast to coast. Later 'Hadrian's Wall,' built AD 122. One mile away...The Castrum etc, is now part of UNESCO World Heritage, and an active Archaeological site.

ASPECTS
OF
LOVE

THE SONG OF THE NIGHTINGALE

A deep tranquillity had charmed that summer night,

And wrapped us in a silken skein of dreams…

The scent of you beside me filled my head…

While glowing moonlight wakened into life

A million jasmine blossoms, breathing love…

Then into this enchantment burst a song…

A wordless anthem, cascading pure delight.

Like fluid gold it flooded the silent air,

With spontaneous cadences of natural exultation

Trilled into the emptiness, until the emptiness was filled.

And suddenly it seemed the Earth stood still,

To better hear that fledgling from God's choir.

You stirred in sleep, and smiled within your dreams…

While liquid harmony encompassed those dark, night hours,

As that sweet songbird, all unseen and shadowy,

Poured forth his glorious carillon of joy.

It was an unscripted creation, engendered in starlight,

By one whose joyous gifts o'er flowed his soul…

The unseen singer craved no audience, save for the starry sky,

As he chimed his heavenly aria robed in leaves…

It was no dream… but while that small bird sang,

The bird became the music… the music… the night.

The smiling moon paused… lingered long on high,

Drew closer to our window and gazed in…

Caressed your sleeping eyes, your hair, and lips…

Before that glorious singer left, to sing again …

For other ears… Or carol close to heaven.

WHERE THE RIVER BENDS

I know a place, just where the river bends,

A place of loveliness, outside of time,

Where silver willows bow to the water's edge,

And swallows dart along its peaceful flow.

There, spotted trout lurk by the shadowy stones,

And droning bees go lumbering flower to flower,

Plundering the meadow sweet, and columbine,

And tasting each delicate, sun-warmed nectar store.

Entwined on mossy, gold-fringed emerald banks,

Our eager lips first tasted love's sweet joys.

You kissed my hair, and said, the sun lived there,

And that my eyes could drown you in their blue.

So deep the river ran, it overflowed our hearts

With gentle murmurings, and secret songs of love.

They formed our dreams, on floating clouds of gold,

That linger still upon the edges of recall.

Such magic palaces we built, where the river bends,

Sharing our whispered hopes on sun-bright grass…

But though the river flows in timeless flood

Life's seasons flow relentlessly, beyond recall.

Our golden days of Spring burned fast and bright,

And Summer gaily hurried through the years…

Now Autumn's song murmurs with mellow voice,

And from our dreams the swallows have taken flight.

But I recall that place where the river bends,

That place of loveliness, outside of time…

And if our Eldorado still lives there…

Come… Let's reclaim those dreams we still can share.

ETERNAL LOVE

Eternal love... The love which never dies

Survives in faithful constancy

Beneath the darkest skies...

An enduring anchor, weathering the storms of life,

Holding true hearts secure, through tragedy, and strife...

Even, Death, the grim reaper, cannot sever love,

Once the binding of hearts and souls

Is made in Heaven above...

YOUR love... is not lost to me...

Just, briefly... GONE AHEAD...

Still lighting the lonely path which I must tread...

And, as the emptiness of the years I roam,

Your loving spirit walks with me...

To guide me home.

HOME ALONE

Returning home alone, I close the door.

The silence greets me like an empty tomb…

Renewing the pain of your not being there.

Just lonely dust, unstirred, to welcome me!

A million times, and evermore

I find the air unbreathed.

No sound of you to gladden my heavy heart,

Only the empty grate, and silent hollow chair.

The strangled clock marks every futile hour,

Tick-tocking in my heart's locked echoing vault,

Where memories merge into my choking grief,

And suffocate me with their Stygian gloom.

Such is the lingering slipstream of my life…

You are no more… and there is nothing left.

NO TRIVIAL THING

You made of… BETRAYAL, such a trivial thing…

A thoughtless indiscretion of no count!

A brief temptation… meaningless… a minor fall from grace…

No-Harm-Done! BUT no value added for my loyalty, or my heart,

Both casually abandoned for a tempting… fling!

Sincerity, made pointless… for furtive, casual, lust…

Love, is NOT some convenient game we play…

Nor abandoned honour, regained, with a casual shrug…

You made, a straw-hut-fantasy from our love,

Then threw it to the winds, without a thought!

What's done… can never now be… undone…

A house without foundations cannot stand…

Love is no lottery, where tacky tickets say…

Bad luck! No prize… But have another go, another day!

LET DOWN BY LOVE

Why crease your pretty face with futile crying?

Don't think his leaving you has ruined your life.

Just turn your back, and use those feet for walking…

And be glad you never were his bloody wife.

You'll find abundant male-specimens, of our species

Flocking like birds, in every place you go…

You thought you'd found a peacock when you met him…

When what you'd got was really, just a crow!

Maybe you tried too hard… were far too willing?

And like a greedy leech he drained you dry,

That kind of selfishness is not surprising…

But if you want a pig… look in a stye!

Now take this chance, and ask the vital question,

"What DO I want… What is MY life about?"

If you really want someone who *truly* loves you,

Then never settle for a selfish lout!

Find someone with *an honest heart* to give you,

A man who wants to love you… and it shows,

A really grown up, Genuine, Bird of Paradise…

Who stands out, from that selfish horde of crows?

LOVE'S CANZONETTA

Life's voyage is an ocean

Where wrecked hopes and dreams may lie…

But safe from the darkest dangers

Are precious memories which never die.

The benchmarks of our journey

Lie in partings, sorrow-filled…

Of mountains climbed, and pathways taken,

As life's essence is distilled.

When a heart has lost its music

Then life's harmony has gone,

And without love's pulse to cheer it

Life may linger for too long…

Until faint echoes from the past,

And fleeting faces in a dream,

May bring glimpses from life's mirror,

Like blurred shadows in a stream…

And so… the song awakens…

Though it may have slumbered long,

For the loving heart will never

Forget that other heart, where it belongs.

Lost love is not forsaken

As the years drift by and fade,

Its light still shines in Heaven…

For 'tis there that love was made.

OUR SONG

Sing to me again, that song we loved,

For there is old magic, still lingering in the words,

And poignancy, to reawaken the dreams we both once shared.

Let me bathe again in those gentle harmonies,

Which bubbled through our days of happiness.

Sing-back our memories, and brighten these twilight hours

Long faded into silence, beneath times' yellow leaves...

That place, where autumn's footsteps, crushed both flower and fruit

And made of life's vintage, a sour and tasteless wine.

Croon to me softly, in the evening light,

And perfume the world again, with spring-time blooms,

Which languish still, upon the fragrant edge of memory.

Revive the gossamer web of joy around my heart,

And sing to me again, that song we loved.

SEDUCTION

When aging Helen reviewed the indiscretions of her youth,

Was it to Troy or Sparta her thoughts then strayed?

Did any lingering remorseful sighs, regret the pain

Of her abandoned lovers… or of her faithless life?

Lying in flagrante, beneath a languorous moon,

Entwined by silver sea, in passion's glow…

Old Sparta's queen made of seduction a sensuous art…

And launched a thousand reasons for remorse.

What mortal is born, who never hides wild lusts and flaws,

And passionate, dark human frailty, at their core?

Those lingering eruptions from an unrequited heart

Burst ofttimes upon the world, beyond control…

Thus, Paris made of fidelity a facile irrelevance,

When roused in passion, he sought her lips… and Helen smiled.

REMEMBERING YOU

How do I begin to remember you?

I find your smiling eyes and gift of love

In summer's haze, or drifting snowflakes

Falling gently down upon me, from above.

Glimpsed across a room, or shopping in the street…

It is your tender, loving lips I yearn to find and greet.

How do I begin to remember you?

Among the sky-blue violets of another spring?

Or sailing across the summer skies

With swallows on the wing?

I've searched the desolate hours, both night and day,

To find those quiet places where precious memories stay.

How do I begin to remember you?

When autumn leaves fall thick, and skies are grey…

And cold relentless time tears all my dreams away?

Yet, left behind are loving echoes of those last words said…

And mournful anguish in my heart for what is fled…

How do I begin to remember you?...

There is *no end*, to my remembering you!

ASPECTS
OF
NATURE

SUMMER'S ANTHEM

It's June… The days are long the sun is shining.

It's June… The sea is sparkling by the harbour.

Families on holiday,

Pleasure boats around the bay….

And winter's brittle flotsam, lies forgotten…

Summer's Anthem charms life's measure,

And seagulls fill the air with raucous pleasure…

Now merry June is dancing on the seashore…

Once more.

July… The fields of corn wave softly golden.

July… The flowers never bloomed more sweetly.

Colouring each joyful morn

Poppies edge the fields, unshorn…

And all the hedgerows trill a silver chorus.

Song-bird-descants fill the air,

Life and love glow everywhere,

July… The wayside walks and gardens beckon…

Again.

Bright, fickle August trembles with excitement.

Its hedonistic fun beguiles the heart.

Flying high above the crowds

Paper kites and fluffy clouds…

And happy hearts brim full of rapturous pleasure.

Climb a mountain, take a cruise,

Find some shade, and have a snooze…

Romantic August days were made for leisure…
Ever.

Mellow September crowns the summer's bounty,

With russet apples gleaming on the boughs.

Vineyards ripen, honey sweet…

The fruitful season is complete;

For all the summer's luscious gifts are ripened now…

While Nature harmonises a different song,

Now summer's joyful melody has gone.

And the carnival of the year moves gently on…

To autumn's song.

October's languid smile marks summer's passing,

When early frost sharpens the evening air.

Jewelled leaves grow red and die,

When chill winds through the tree-tops sigh,

And the plough turns fertile, brown-ridged furrows now…

Spiders' webs glisten with morning dew,

When October comes to show her sombre hue…

And thus, the year reveals her fading face…

With autumn's race.

MOMENT OF DELIGHT

Here in this breathless hush before the dawn

The stars like flickering candles are snuffed out.

And silently, below the dark sea's rim,

The sun seems loath to rise, on this September morn.

Arched high above the silent un-reaped corn,

The quiet sky cocoons the shadowy fields…

Sweet monkey-musk idles by the trickling rills,

Where clumps of sweet violets sleep on mossy stones…

An early droning bee, probes clover flowers,

And by the coppiced wood a weary fox slinks home.

Tread softly, e'er the slumbering earth awakes,

Go tiptoe in this place of perfect peace…

No Titan voice commands the day to dawn,

No heavenly anthem proceeds the sun's levee…

When suddenly, a silver harmony cleaves the drowsy sky,

And all the birds of heaven rise carolling…

Then from the eastern sea the sun breaks free,

Renewing, with light and life, the waiting earth…

And bringing that rapturous… Moment of Delight…

When self-revealed, shines forth the peaceful glory,

That mystery and splendour… at the dawning of New Day.

THE SEASONS I LOVE

I love the autumn best of all, when leaves turn flamed and gold,

And silver mists drift silently across the mountain fold…

There cattle stand enchanted, half hidden in the lea,

And ancient woodlands breathe the last, of summer's ecstasy…

I love the sounds of winter's blasts, when frost paints hills and fields,

And lacy leaves cling silently, trapped by December's freeze.

Then hips and haws glow, berries red, along the woodland walk,

And Mother Nature rests a while when days are short and dark…

When dainty spring comes dancing, who does not love her smile?

She frolics over woods and fields, all clothed in green, the while.

Around her feet bright flowers are strewn; the trees are decked in May,

While swallows glide the riverbanks, to watch the lambs at play….

Majestic summer moves with pride, and sweeps across the land,

The days are long, the skies are blue… life blooms at his command.

Rich, glowing gifts, touch every heart… who could not love this king?

His bounty brings the harvest home, and makes the songbirds sing…

But I love autumn best of all, the closing of the year,

When Nature draws her tapestry around her like a fur.

Then little grey things hide their stores, against the winter sleep,

And the spangled heavens glow silently… before the frosts bite hard and deep,

WILD BLACKBERRIES

Let me taste once again wild blackberries,

Plucked with purple fingers from the vines

That tangled where the coal trucks used to roll

Down the abandoned, rusty, iron tracks

So overgrown and lost, that only children knew

Where to creep, carefully, through the thorns.

Our roaming had few limits. Summer took us far

Across the whiskered, golden barley fields,

To tunnel where the rabbits' burrows ran

Among the corn stooks, near the railway's edge.

Or lie in deep, fragrant hay, and watch the larks

Spiral, with crystal song towards the clouds

That floated overhead, like ice-cream foam.

We knew the secret pool at Spion Kop,

Where foxes lapped, and cubs romped with the frogs…

In silence, we knew how to wait and watch

The wonders which unfolded every day.

Those summers seemed to own no rain-swept skies,

Our days were golden, endless, and carefree.

Autumn brought orchards full of sun-sweet fruits,

Conkers and puffballs… all for our delight!

When winter filled the fields for snow-ball fights,

We'd build our crooked snowmen, with cold hands,

And stamp our icy feet to tingling warmth…

Await the thaw, and suck on icicles

That grew mysteriously, in those winter nights

When Jack-Frost painted all the windowpanes,

And breath hung, like a wreath, around our downy heads.

We'd watch the falling stars at winter's end…

The last white furrows underneath the hedge,

Then count the lambs, when flickering spring returned,

And snowdrops bloomed along the woodland ride.

Soft, hatching, budding things, proclaimed life was renewed.

Bright willows shimmered grey, where the stream flowed.

There we would splash, and kick the water into arcs

Of glittering jewels, and rainbow-filled cascades.

The song that Nature sang filled all our days…

We heard the rhythm of life's music in our ears…

Let me taste once again, wild blackberries…

Plucked with purple fingers from the vines

That tangled where the coal-trucks used to roll…

THE MARIGOLDS

I still recall the old house on the cliffs…

The coastguard lived there many years ago,

Until a century of progress cancelled out the need,

And left the winter storms to do their worst.

Then came the time the house fell derelict.

The neglected garden faded… overgrown and lost…

But every year the marigolds still tossed their shaggy heads,

Against the onslaught of the screaming gulls…

Rain soaked and battered, when the sea-squalls lashed the shore.

The time came when wild campion and sea-thrift,

Spread in profusion where the house had been,

Yet still the marigolds tenaciously bloomed on…

Unloved, uncared for… but surviving all

That man, and nature, could ever throw at them.

The North winds tore the roots from each sweet rose,

And withered every other living thing…

But still, unconquered seeds of tufted gold,

Beneath the turf lay hid from autumn gales.

And from that once bought sixpenny packet, came

An annual golden sheaf of brazen blooms…

Perhaps some future trippers to the coast

Will eat their cake and sandwiches, and turn

Their sandy feet towards that desolate place…

And wonder how those golden flowers grow,

Unconquered, resilient blooms, against the sea.

GREY SQUIRRELS

The leaves are rustling where the squirrels play

Darting like shadows through the canopy…

Grey into grey, and russet into green.

Cavorting between the seasons… spirits of air...

Their silent scampering, dapples the spring-time light…

Fearless, those nimble-footed wraiths play up and down the boughs.

Fast, furious, sleek, sure-footed, foraging, and coy…

Tangling with sinuous pleasure through the pines,

Bright bead-black eyes forever on alert…

Crouched at an elevated meal… or upside down!

Clinging with needle claws to gnaw their feast…

Then frolicking blithely, leapfrogging down the lawn…

Or racing again for safety in the leaves…

Life in the fast lane… satisfies their needs.

THE SCARECROW

I'm called an old scarecrow, an object of scorn,

Just Farmer's off-casts, stuffed with corn.

Arms without hands, sleeves threadbare…

Head without knowledge, envy, or care.

Hung like a flag on a broken mast…

Abandoned to every seasonal blast…

Scorched by the sun and soaked by the rain,

Alone and solitary here I remain.

My home in the field is without child or spouse,

But would I change places, and live in a house?

Four walls make a prison, while here free I stand

Benevolently gazing across open land.

Nature stirs all around me, and from it I learn

All through the year, as the four seasons turn.

Birds in my pockets build nests of hay,

And I shelter their fledglings till they fly away.

Secrets aplenty from fieldmouse and hare,

Are whispered to me in the cool midnight air.

I can never repeat them, for tongueless I stand…

Nodding and waving, across the farmland.

LATE SUPPER

My sole companion in the dead of night

A mesmerised gecko, offended by the beam

Cast by the torch I'd used, to read the time…

So late! So early! Not much past two-thirty…

Reflective eyes alive there in the dark,

Waiting, and watching for what else might stir

With wings or stings. The lurking hunter clung

Just where the curtain pole and mosquito netting met,

Shocked that a shaft of light had found him out…

Betrayed his subterfuge, revealed his silent pose

Above my bed. The buzz of a mosquito

Suddenly stopped… A downy moth went crazy,

Spiralling round and round… bemused and frail.

Then darkness followed, when I switched out the light,

And curtains descended for the fated pair.

The gecko vanished into the silent hour,

His dining satisfied… His dignity restored…

And I slept peacefully until the sun came up,

Pestered by no other intruders in the night.

SUNSET

Soft as the sigh of the cool west wind,

Shrouded around by night…

Through the portal of flaming clouds

The dying sun sinks out of sight.

A vanquished monarch's last farewell

Kisses the gold-drenched grass…

One heavenly moment on Earth, before

The shadows lengthen… the glories pass.

ASPECTS

OF

LIFE

A FIRESIDE TALE

(Spoken by Four, Northumbrian Voices)

Male voice…

A fisher-wife once lived in Cullercoats,

A comely woman… pillar of her church.

She had but one son, James… her only joy.

A braw, brave and a bonny lad he was.

From childhood he had sailed the coble-boats,

Alongside his father… learned the fishers' craft.

The sea was in his blood, he knew no fear…

To be a fisherman his one desire,

And live in Cullercoats his only dream.

Female voice…

Their peaceful days came to a cruel end,

When war-clouds overshadowed all the land.

The fisher-wife was grieved, when he was called

To be a naval rating in that war.

Her heart was overwhelmed with fear and dread…

But she had faith and trusted in her prayers.

God was her refuge in her time of need,

The saints would keep James safe, and bring him home.

Male voice

All through the Kaiser's war James fought at sea,

Right bravely… and won medals in the fray.

The war kept him from home for four long years,

Crossing the oceans, serving his country's need.

His letters told how much he missed his home,

That he was well… And she was dearly loved.

He wrote of battles that his ship had fought…

He'd been at Scapa Flow, with Jellicoe,

And fought at Jutland, 'gainst the German Fleet.

Then Armistice was signed… Great God be praised!

The war was ended, soon James would come home.

When all the guns fell silent, James' ship sailed,

To bring him home, and light her life again.

Female voice

Most tragically the vessel it was lost,

Somewhere beneath the North Atlantic deeps…

It struck a floating mine and quickly sank,

"Lost with all hands," the official papers said…

She couldn't read the telegram for tears…

Would not believe the words, when she was told…

Ran screaming from the house like one possessed.

Tearing her hair she fled into the church,

Distraught, she knelt before the altar rail…

Wringing her hands, beseeching Heaven to hear.

Wife… (pleading and with emotion)

"Dear Father, let him live… Let James come home!

He is the only joy you've given to me.

I beg you not to part me from my son.

Dear God, please give him back and let him live."

Male voice

The hollow building echoed to her prayer,

As over and again she said the words.

But never an answering word came from on high…

No angel flew to Earth to comfort her.

The church lay silent, no one heard her plea.

The saints stood in their niches deaf and dumb…

And parson was far away across the fells,

Visiting the farms, before the snows set in.

Female voice

They found her in the dark at even-tide,

Prostrate and cold upon the altar steps…

Scarcely alive, her heart-beat fluttering faint.

Her husband carried her home, fearing she would die.

Her heart was broken… she'd no will to live.

Her mind unhinged by her most grievous loss,

She fell into a fever of the brain…

Rambling in her talk, no longer sane.

Her husband, good man that he was, he tried

To comfort her… but nothing quenched her pain,

So sunken was she in her black despair,

Raving she'd never again see her dear boy.

In melancholic grief she wept and pined…

Until her husband and her friends believed

That she would die, before the year's end came.

Male voice

All winter long he nursed her, kept her safe,

And tried to cheer her heart, and make her smile.

They'd sit together warm beside the fire…

But all the light that lit her eyes had died.

Her hair had lost its sheen, and when she spoke

Her voice was feeble, like a little child.

Her husband was gentle with her, did his best,

But it was clear, her soul was in decline.

Wife (weakly and confused)

"I heard a wailing in the air last night."

Husband (kindly)

"Dear lass… you heard the wind across the moor."

Wife (Startled)

"Who comes a-tapping at the windowpane?"

Husband

"It's but the rattling rain… and nothing more."

Wife (tearfully)

"Someone lies hiding, spying by the gate."

Husband (trying to cheer her up)

"There's nothing near the gate, but yellow furze,

You used to dye James' pace-eggs with the flowers.

D'ye not ken how he liked bright-coloured eggs?

You'd wrap old onion skins around them tight,

And boil them, so they'd come out golden brown."

Wife (in a resigned voice)

"When Easter comes, James will be safely home.

And I will boil him coloured pace-eggs, like before."

Female voice

She twined her arms around her knees, and rocked

Backward and forth upon the creaking stool…

Picturing those happy days when he was young.

They seemed like some faint dream from long ago.

Wife(sadly)

"Today while I was baking, the fire was quenched,

And all my batch of "singin' hinnies" was spoilt."

Husband (gently)

"The rain came down the chimney, bonny lass,

And water drenched the coals… the fire went out.

What makes you fear someone is taunting you?"

Wife (tearfully)

"Because God has forsaken me… turned His back…

And now the Devil's imps tease me each day…

The war is over… James SHOULD BE at home…

'Tis God-Himself, that keeps my bairn away!

I pleaded for His help… HE closed His ears…"

(She begins to weep)

Husband (softly to console her)

"It grieves my heart, dear lass, to see you sad…

James is not hidden… our son is dead and gone!

We have our memories from happier times.

God did not choose to bring this grief on you…

One day, we both will see his face again."

Female voice

She covered up her ears and screamed and cried.

Wife (confused and angry)

"I will not hear you say my James is dead!

He's on the sea somewhere… and coming home.

Sometimes I hear his footsteps on the path…

But when I run to see, they draw him back,

And keep him hidden, to hold him from my side."

Husband (sadly and softly to calm her)

"There are no footsteps on the gravel path…

You hear the crashing waves down by the shore."

Wife (eagerly)

"Today I found some seashells on the step…
James always brings me shells when he comes home…"

Husband (interrupting her)

"Those shells are old… they've lain there many years,
He brought them from the beach when he was small."

Wife (excitedly, ignoring him)

"Husband… I KNOW our boy will soon come home…"

Husband (trying to calm her)

"He cannot come, sweet lass, he's fathoms deep."

Wife (excitedly, still ignoring him)

"I've made his feather bed… it's soft for his return…
Surely, he WILL be back when Easter comes."

Husband (sadly and resigned)

"How CAN he come… when death has closed his eyes?"

Wife (shouting angrily)

"HE DOES NOT SLEEP, and soon he will be here!"

Male voice

In such mad grieving, slowly the dark days passed... *(pauses)*

The autumn and winter brought rough seas and gales…

The coble-boats could seldom put to sea…

The fishing was poor… the herring shoals stayed off

Feeding in water deeper than men could fish.

Then came a turning of the wrecking winds…

The herring at last came closer to the shore.

Out on the cliffs the lookouts ran to tell,

Great silver swathes were feeding close in-shore.

The fishermen prepared to go and bring them in…

Great God be praised… the herring shoals were back!

The coble boats sailed out to fish the banks,

And Cullercoats bustled with the silver-darlings once more!

Female voice

That herring-harvest was the best for years,

And heavy creels of fish were brought ashore.

The women gathered when the boats came in,

Their gutting knives already sharp and bright…

It was their work, to split and salt the catch,

Prepare the fish, and fill the smoke-house racks.

The smell of smouldering oak-chips fumed the air,

Curing those laden catches from the sea.

The women toiled till dark down on the beach,

Scraping the scaly herring every day…

Their stinking clothes splattered with silver scales,

Their hands red-raw, from wind and brine and fish.

But there was happy laughter on the shore,

For hard work was the only life they knew.

Then cured and boxed the kippers were carted south…

Such was the way the fishers earned their pay.

Male voice

The fisher-wife walked endlessly alone,

Shunning all company, work, and village life.

The anguished weeks had brought a gloomy change…

An air of darkness hung about her now.

She seldom said a word to anyone…

Neglected her wifely duties every day.

Wandered instead, upon the cliffs or shore…

Listening for voices whispering on the wind…

Seeking mysterious messages none could give…

Female voice

When Shrovetide and Lent were ended, church bells rang.

The nave was decked in brightest spring-time flowers...

Easter had come, and Christ the Lord was risen!

The Cullercoats' fisher-folk sang joyfully in praise.

The Harvest of the Sea, His bounteous gift,

Had filled their nets... They gladly sang and prayed.

Male voice

Each year at Easter time, a pedlar came,

With laden baskets, tricked out with pretty things...

Then all the village buzzed, with laughing wives,

And dancing maids, flocking to buy such treats...

Male and female voices (alternately with excitement)

"A ribbon for the hair... a length of lace,

"A tin-plate toy... A bobbin of silk thread;

"Pearl buttons for a waistcoat, newly stitched,

"A dainty collar of embroidered voile,

"New cuffs to brighten up a tired gown,

"A measuring-tape hidden in a white whalebone,

"Red spotted kerchief... combs to hold the hair..."

Female voice (interrupting)

The good man tried to tempt his wife with treats,

But she just shook her head, and dumbly stared…

Until she spied a pennywhistle, shine

Beneath the gaudy ribbons, and twists of lace.

That was the ONLY thing her heart desired.

Her boy had often played, to make her smile.

He'd pipe a jig, or rousing marching song…

Her soulful eyes begged only one penny piece…

Her one desire, to learn to pipe a tune.

Male voice

Her husband could not deny such simple joy…

And gladly bought the penny pipe for her.

Then with a kiss bestowed the favoured toy…

Told her she was his own fair, bonny lass.

It pleased him well that she should want to play.

He'd give the world… if only she would smile…

Female voice

The fisher-wife went wandering on the shore.

She cared not what the other women said.

They had their bairns about them, safe at home…

She only a gnawing emptiness in her breast.

Each day she paced the lower ebb-tide reach,

That lay beyond the turning tidal flow.

Her neighbours marked her aimless wanderings,

Unhinged by grief, and muttering to herself.

Pausing each now and then to face the wind,

Turn to each quarter, North, South, West, and East…

Blow shrilly on her pipe, some strange harsh tune…

Pause… listen intently… cast her gaze to sea,

Willing her dear, sweet boy to come to her.

Male voice

For seven long days she scarcely left the shore,

Keeping her lonely vigil night and day…

Until her husband questioned why she stayed

So long out of the house, and by the sea?

Wife (in a simple matter-of-fact voice)

"I'm whistling up a wind, to bring James home."

Male voice

She answered simply, turning her mournful gaze.

Husband (deeply concerned)

"God-help-us! Woman… when will this madness end?

No fisher-woman whistles for the wind!

Such wicked business stands against God's laws…

The dead must rest in peace, until He calls!

'Tis by God's Grace some sleep in hallowed ground…

And many-a fisherman rests beneath the sea…

God gives them each a place to lie, and wait,

Do not oppose that AWFUL, solemn law!

For nothing but evil comes from such a deed…"

Wife (shrilly with rising anger)

"What care I for God's Laws? I seek my child…

And I will whistle till he comes to me.

I've lived my life in keeping with God's Will,

And bowed my head to every burden given…

ONE child alone, was all the joy I knew…

I Will Not yield him up to Hell, or Heaven!

If God wills that my only son be dead…

Then I am left to make a Devil's pact!

So, James may be with me and I with him…

I care not for the laws of God or man…

I'll whistle in every quarter, at low tide,

For I believe he'll hear his mother's call.

North, South, East, West, my son WILL hear my cry…

He'll come to me again, though God forbids…"

(She changes her tone… now, softly and with affection)

"He was a good bairn… always came when called…

No matter how far… nor what the game he played…

And now he will NOT fail to heed my pipe,

Keening into the wind, to beckon him…

(With rising determination and power)

Oh! I *will* whistle, loud as Gabriel's horn,

And James will hear me, with his loving heart…

Through storm or tempest, he will find a way…

Though legions of devils, bar the way… HE'LL COME!

He will not keep from me, and see me pine…

Full seven tides I've whistled for the wind,

And seven times I've cursed the heavens on high…

Broken the Holy Laws, that fisher-folk all keep…

(Shrilly, and in tearful desperation)

So…Come He-Must… OR I WILL DROWN AT SEA!"

Husband (deeply distressed… trying to calm her)

"Dear wife, why must you seek to fight God's will?

Our son lies lost… his soul has gone from him.

He cannot waken now till Judgement Day…

His bones are whitened, in his deep-sea grave."

Wife (forcefully, and with angry determination)

"Then I will whistle till the Devil hears…

I'll pipe and whistle, face whatever comes.

Between the tides, I'll hunt... till Hell is breached…

Do WHAT I MUST… I've sworn to find my boy…"

Male voice

When dawn's first rays, came glimmering in the sky,

She quietly stole across the silent shore,

And loosed James' coble-boat into the tide…

Hoisted the flapping sail to catch the wind,

Then sailed, fearless of danger, alone and out to sea.

A light breeze ruffled white caps on the waves,

As into the mist, the fisher-wife steered far.

No one saw any sign of how she left…

Her good man slept, so lightly did she leave…

An evil wind came whistling from the North,

And carried her beyond the harbour bar.

She steadied the boat, and shrieked into the wind…

Wife (shrieking madly)

"Hear me! Dear lad… I've come to call you back!

Rise-up, come sit beside me, and we'll sail…

For I am willing to leave this world behind,

And roam the seas with you, beyond God's Grace.

For you… I'll forfeit my immortal soul,

Relinquish Salvation… sup with the Devil himself,

And be an outcast… till Eternity!"

Female voice

She lashed the sail, and took the pipe again,

Whistling her strange tune wildly to the sky.

Tumultuous waves rose high… wild storm-clouds surged,

As though in answer to her anguished plea.

Tears streamed down from her eyes till she was blind.

The tossing boat ploughed swiftly on its way,

Carrying her afar on mountainous waves…

But piping madly, she felt naught of fear.

Fair visions of her son were in her mind,

She felt his presence, singing in the storm.

A pall of weird, blue lightning struck the boat…

Her loosened hair streamed out into the wind.

Then in a phosphorescent flash, she saw

James' smiling face, all strange and ghastly white,

Rising towards her, from the hellish deeps…

Reaching to touch her where she sat.

Wife (grief-stricken and tearful)

"Oh son! Dear son… come to your mother's arms,

As once you did, when you were but a child…"

Male voice (interrupting)

High on the cliffs, men hunting watched the scene.

The parson, the farmer, and the local squire…

They, hurrying homeward, to escape the storm,

High, from the headland, witnessed what befell.

Watched through a spyglass the grim sights at sea…

Transfixed, but too far off to render help…

No means lay anywhere, to save those souls… (*pause…sadly*)

When all had passed too far for mortal help,

They hurried home agog, to tell their tale…

A coble heading outward, northward driven,

Its red sail set full-on into the storm.

Making no effort to turn for leeward shores,

Seeming to steer a course straight for Hell's mouth…

Dangerously buffeted by the Devil's own glee…

Driven on, as they could see, without remorse.

Cape Horn could never have raged a wilder sea.

Hell's maw gaped wide, to draw the coble in…

While stinking, sulphurous fumes, poisoned the air.

And strangely to their eyes, they each agreed…

At first there was but ONE, who manned the oars,

Then, of-a-sudden, TWO sat side by side,

Both rowing, oblivious of those monstrous waves,

And keeping their steady unison, all unfazed…

Pulling in rhythm, easy and content,

Skimming the angry seas as in a skiff…

Laughing as though they picnicked on a lake.

Seated in mortal danger without a care…

A woman, with a young man at her side,

Bathed in a strange, and eerie, livid glow…

That spoke, to those who watched, of some strange power

Drawing the tragic pair, on to their fate.

Female voice

The parson spent long hours upon his knees

Praying for both those souls lost to the sea.

But village folk said, it was the Devil's work…

And all the Cullercoats fisher-folk agreed…

No Godly woman whistles for a wind

To change the natural order wrought by death…

Such wickedness denies God's Holy Will…

And those who bargain for the Devil's boon,

Pay with their immortal souls… The Devil's price.

Male voice

The strange story was told, down through the years

By witnesses of worth, who'd seen those things.

No answers were found to solve the strange affair…

No bodies floated home, to any shore…

No wreckage of the coble… EVER found.

Female voice

Some said that James came back… to ease her grief!

Some vowed her whistling opened Hell's grim gates…

But many of the fisher-folk believe

To whistle the Devil's wind, flies in God's face…

To cheat the dead their grave…. is mortal sin….

(Sea-sounds, and seagulls calling… fading out)

WHERE SOFTLY STEALS THE NIGHT

Dark halls of the Alhambra, marbled and mystical by moonlight,

Where splashing fountains cascade in sparkling rills, sweetening the summer air,

And damask petals, from the Sultan's roses perfume the quiet hours…

Beyond these pleasure courts of opulence, the flowers of Earth vie with the stars of heaven.

Now, in the sultry darkness, Granada's rippling roofs lie calm and still.

And conjured by the moonbeams' spell, dark passionate eyes glitter

Through the jalousies of the lattice screens, upon this gift from Heaven…

Where softly steals the night…

Midnight enchantments stir, wreathing the high Nevada's silver crown, with wisps of gossamer clouds

That trail above the downward rushing streams, to dance in wild flamencos,

Urging faint, ghostly shadows into life, cajoling them to quit their dark cloisters,

And taste the shimmering starlight, of the Andalusian night…

Below Granada's towers the waiting Vega trembles into life…

Stirred by melancholy chords strummed on a lone guitar…

And heels rapping their passionate responses to staccato castanets….

Where softly steals the night.

Listen with your heart if you would hear, faint echoes, stirring up the long dead past…

Whispers among the orange blossoms, murmuring of heavenly hours, romanced in sweetness

By concubines, with silver lutes… and languid with songs of love,

Charming the Sultan's care-worn soul, to bring him fleeting dreams of Paradise.

Or glimpse dark shadows, pungent with sweat and treachery, crouched in the Lion Court,

Nursing honed scimitars, bright as lovers' eyes, and poised to stain the pristine marble red…

Yet swifter than a stolen moonlight kiss… this phantom cavalcade flits on its shadowy way,

Where softly steals the night.

Dark halls of the Alhambra, marbled and mystical by moonlight…

At dawn your pageant fades, its ghostly banners fleeing before the sun…

Retreating into the misty embrace of night… Huyen las sombras ante la luz!

The harsh Andalusian light too cruel and bright, for tremulous shades, who crave

Only the quiet magic of the moon. There in sequestered avenues they live on,

Tiptoeing where purple shadows dream, and gentle waters flow...

Those ghostly revellers dance-on, each summer night

Among the Alhambra's quiet courts and fragrant paths...

Where softly steals the night.

NO REHEARSAL: NO ENCORE.

Life's an unscripted play, without a plot,

An improvisation where we strive to change

Our disappointing parts for finer roles…

Frantically scrambling up the greasy pole,

While struggling with the awkward scenes we didn't plan…

Our fanciful illusions mock reality,

Jumbling the brain with vanity and power.

We yearn for finer robes which don't quite fit,

Jewels, and trinkets… and mouth false cut-glass vowels,

Bemused by the notion that the outward show

Is closer to reality, than the inner truth.

But face-the-mirror, wipe the greasepaint clean,

And leave revealed the naked self within…

It's a dull canvas upon which to form your dreams.

Truth can be masked, and hidden under lies…

Covered by layered facades and gaudy fripperies…

Constructed by deceivers, to deceive,

But no permanent hindrance done to the pretentious show…

Each day the overture ends, the curtain rises up…

And so, the devious interactions begin again…

We dodge and weave through life's course, day by day

Bumbling about, or strutting a puffed-up part,

Mouthing whatever words best suit the theme...

It's all a pretence... sly eyes, and flaccid lying lips,

Moist sweaty skin, or grasping lecherous hands...

No maquillage obliterates these flaws...

Yet every player strutting on life's stage

Joins happily in this game of self-deceit,

Fluffing each punchline of the denouement scenes...

Stand up, fall-down... play president or clown,

With envy or loathing... or poison every part...

It's certain many roles will come our way,

As we negotiate our straight or crooked paths.

We mime our deepest griefs; soliloquise our fears,

And wrestle with love or conflict, when they strike,

Shuffling about, or sucking our wet thumbs...

Moaning of this or that when we have failed.

Yet comprehending, too late, bad choices made...

The chances missed... the love songs never sung!

Venting our futile angst against the gods,

That squat like three sad monkeys, on a shelf

In some unfathomable celestial paradise...

And are we blind, and deaf and dumb, to tragic woes

That never touch the nerves of our own skin?

Events which remain remote... while hell goes trundling past,

For those believers who thought that someone cared?

It's ever been like this since time began…

The Comedy; The Tragedy; The Farce:

There's no stage-door to Heaven… no back-way-in,

No great director god, lurking in the wings

Cheering us on, and promising us… *finer future roles*…

Or wiping our snivelling noses each time we fail…

No green room for a respite… save the tomb…

Life is no rehearsal… This act is *for real*…

How long you'll ride this bubble… who can tell?

MRS NEMO'S NEMESIS

Mrs Nemo was a lady, widowed and alone,

Who supported herself with paying guests in her home.

The hand-printed notice on her welcoming door

Said, "QUIET ROOM TO LET, B&B, ON THE FIRST FLOOR."

Her clientele were *commercials*, with a regular beat,

Who found parking easy on Adelaide Street.

She preferred that her guests were quiet and refined,

But turned no one away who was spiritually inclined.

Her House-Rules were simple… "Please leave shoes in the hall…

"No smoking; No drinking; No loud music at all…

"Breakfast at seven; vacate rooms by nine,

"And please give me notice if intending to dine."

Mrs Nemo's interests were all, of… *the spiritual kind*

And she endeavoured to keep all her chakras aligned…

She meditated daily, for the insight it brought…

But the opening of her *third eye* was what she'd long sought!

Evening classes and books… she'd given them a try,

But nothing had succeeded in opening her *third eye*.

It continued the elusive desire of her brain,

Until Mr Ajuna turned up in the rain.

It was a quiet Sunday evening with no cars in the street,

And she'd just fed her cat, with tinned salmon as a treat...

She peeped through the curtains when she heard the doorbell

And pursed her lips... "Someone with something to sell?"

A sharp glint of suspicion flashed through her eyes...

When she noticed his suitcase... Like a coffin in size!

She opened the door, just an inch, cautiously,

And Mr Ajuna bowed low graciously.

He was wearing a turban and long robes of green...

The most impressive foreign gentleman she'd ever seen...

Not very tall, but commanding and bright

He stood clearly revealed in the yellow streetlight.

"Dear madam, I have come at your earnest request,

Because you have need of a gentleman guest."

"Oh dear!" She said flustered, "There's been some mistake,

"It's really only weekday commercials I take."

"No mistake, dear lady," Ajuna replied,

Gazing deep and intently straight into her eyes.

"The heavens have decreed you're in need of my aid,

"And to open your *third eye*, I have come, all unpaid.

"Your prayers have been granted, and here I now stand,

"I have come, as your guru, from a far distant land."

He spoke so politely… looking honest and neat,

That she opened the door and brought him in from the street.

His robes were quite dry despite heavy evening rain…

And his oversized luggage, likewise, was the same.

It astonished Mrs Nemo when he called it, to come,

And it glided obediently into the room.

"That's a wonderful suitcase you've got, Mr … er?"

"Oh! Just call me, Ajuna… it's what I prefer.

"And I'll call you, *Memsahib*… if you wouldn't mind,

"Because you're a lady… of the upper-class kind."

Mrs Nemo was flattered, and went weak at the knees,

She felt flustered, and excited, and eager to please.

She brought him some tea and fussed with the fire…

To have her *own guru*, fulfilled every desire!

"Do you think you'll stay long? You must have second sight!

"And, in spite-of-the-rain, and on such a wet night…

"Anyone would imagine you hadn't come far…."

He interrupted, "Memsahib, as a guru… I travel *by star*!

"Ajuna knows all the wise secrets on Earth,

"And with me to instruct you… you'll achieve *your rebirth*.

"When you're ready, we'll begin with an O of B.E…

"That's an Out-Of-Body-Experience, to gurus like me.

"I will teach you to leave your Earth Body behind,

"And fly through the Cosmos, using only your mind!"

She was deeply impressed, and showed him around,

And he trotted behind, never making a sound.

From the hall to the attic, they looked everywhere.

"Now I feel I am ready," she said, as they came down the stair.

Back in the lounge, he went down on one knee,

And gazed in her eyes, telling her he could see

That she was an *old soul*, from his own ancient land,

And the moment had come, for *her-inner-eye,* to expand…

"I am going to show you where true wisdom lies…

"Just keep breathing quietly and look deep in my eyes.

"The third eye, when it opens, brings contentment and peace,

"And infinite wisdom, and spiritual release…

"Now sleeeep… Mrs Nemo, as never before,

"Let your inner-eye open its wonderful door…"

He fixed her attention with a hypnotic stare,

And she instantly went limp… and slid off her chair!

Mrs Nemo awoke on the sofa next day

To find Mr Ajuna quite vanished away.

Gone were her pearls, and her family's treasure,

Gone her TV, and credit cards for good measure.

Everything portable, and easily turned into cash,

Had been spirited away in his coffin-filled stash.

While she'd slept Ajuna, and his suitcase, hadn't lingered,

He'd even removed the gold rings from her fingers!

The enlightenment she'd hoped for, inside of her head

Had just been a dream… Now she wished she was dead!

The coffin-sized suitcase, and its owner were gone,

On the legs of an accomplice, inside all along.

The police caught them boarding a plane bound for Spain,

Where they planned to continue their nefarious game…

Some of her goods were recovered and returned,

But Mrs Nemo realised that from the experience she HAD learned…

She took a week's holiday down by the sea,

And resolved nevermore to invite strangers for tea.

No sweet-talking foreigner would again mess with her mind…

And *her third eye* was shut… and staying permanently blind!

THE WISE WOMAN SPEAKS

"I never planned to be a matriarch,
Nor any of the changes of my life.
Now, in the inner sanctum of my mind
The girl I was, looks out upon the world,
Then meets the conflict, of the mirror's truth.

"I scarcely marked the milestones of my life,
While they were sketched in hopeful green and gold…
And never saw myself as… *growing old;*
Sunrise to sunset the years all treacle-trickled by,
In scrabbling for survival and tinkering with life.

"I've known both birth and death, and all between,
And touched the heights of heaven, and depths of hell…
Filling my cup of sorrow many times,
When fate has blindly pointed this way or that…
Such paths I trod I rather would have left.

"Somewhere the fates contrived my lifetime's span…
But knowing nothing of my journey's length
I sought no short-cuts, in survival's game,

And never tried to walk in other shoes

Than those I wore, upon my own two feet.

"And as for love… that glorious, painful, fire…

That drives us often onto madness' rim …

It burns the brightest when its fierce flames cool,

And serves us best when all its smoke has cleared,

And only the glowing embers yet remain.

"Of me, I would not ever have it said…

"'She was too timid to live… too afeared to die…'"

We pass each stage of life with changing roles,

Confronting whatever trials may come our way…

This is the total wisdom of my years."

THE CLOWN

Drums roll, the band strikes up, the curtains part…
And out I tumble… falling on my face,
With balloons and feathers, mask of red and white...
The maquillage I've worn for fifty years.
I spring alive when once the children laugh,
To see me roll and caper in sawdust…
But slap the sticks, and trip a merry dance…
Then tiptoe over everything that's real.

Beneath the artiste's mask there breathes a man…
Blundering around in life, bemused and old…
Shrivelled to a tragic joke… a foolish tale
Written on banana skins, and old billboards.
Perhaps the world is full of clowns like me,
Faded and peeling, living their cardboard lives?
But slap the sticks, and trip a merry dance,
Then tiptoe over everything that's real.

I touched on love once, when I still was young,
Found Columbine, who graced my salad days…
Her laughter rippled gaily through my soul,

And tempted me to leave the empty stage…

We seldom recognise Dame Fortune's gifts,

Until like summer swallows they've all flown…

But slap the sticks, and trip a merry dance,

Then tiptoe over everything that's real.

Playing the Fool, is all a clown can do,

With grotesque mouth, huge feet, and ginger wig…

Stand up…Fall-down… Shine in the spotlight's glare…

But *who* is the *real* clown… me, or the mask I wear?

Sometime the show must end… *the truth* be told…

Then out of my baggy suit I'll step, and leave…

Remove the painted mask… the wig and boots,

Wave one… *Goodbye*… and bow as life's curtains close.

But slap the sticks, and trip a merry dance,

Then tiptoe over everything that's real.

CYPRESS TREES

In the languid heat of the Spanish afternoon,

When the lemon trees droop, tired as burdened mules,

The blind accordionist finds shelter in their shade,

And hangs his head, in quiet, easy sleep.

A lean white cat paws at a shrivelled leaf,

Where a cicada chirps, and springs from certain death.

Such is siesta, not a bird is heard…

The graveyard on the hill, has come to town…

Where the cypress trees point solemnly at heaven.

When the belfry's tuneless clock disturbs his rest,

The accordionist shakes off his weariness,

And runs his nimble fingers through his hair.

As the silent dusk gathers, women emerge to gossip,

Leaning against their sun-bleached kitchen doors.

In his black hat, and weedy dust-stained gown,

The clerigo chivvies children at their play…

And on the quiet hill, the cypress trees mournfully

Maintain their twilight vigil, under heaven.

The cool of night descends, with breezes from the hills,

And the scent of lemon flowers breathes in the darkened air.

The accordionist lays bare his anguished soul,

With mournful dirges, welcoming the night.

Only the silent shadows witness his laments,

And the ghosts of days forgotten, see him weep.

Deaf to his plaintive airs, the moonlight gazes down,

And the weary cypress trees sigh, by the cemetery walls,

Unmoved by those desolate, human sorrows in the night.

Suddenly a cacophony of strumming guitars

Silences that mournful, lachrymose lament,

And the streets erupt with hurrying, jostling feet

As the air begins to throb with merriment...

Doors are flung wide... A Fiesta bursts upon the night...

And young and old hasten, to celebrate life's joyful flight...

Passionate eyes glitter... feet dance in the moonlight's glow...

Whirling until the pavements sing... and the echoes resound...

There, where the patient cypress trees wait...

Quietly thronging the hill-road... to oblivion.

WITNESS FOR THE DEFENCE

Voices; Narrator: Defendant:

Witness: Judge.

Narrator

The days of the trial were ending. Only one defence witness to hear,

The courtroom was electric with tension, waiting for the judge to appear.

With stumbling steps, the defendant was brought to her place in the dock,

Then the jury filed in, eyes averted from the accused in her little black frock.

Resembling a gathering of vultures, the lawyers adjusted their gowns,

They were grim faced, but sure that the verdict would soon send the guilty one down.

The air crackled hostile with hatred, for the evil deed she had done,

And they'd painted the face of, *Lucrezia*, while she'd stood in the dock deaf and dumb.

In judicial robes of scarlet, the judge solemnly considered the scene,

He'd observed the defendant minutely, and his instincts were troubling him.

His impartiality was paramount. A judge must delve deep for the truth,

Explore all possible mitigation and question the burden of proof.

The evidence from prosecuting counsel was unequivocal… a man was dead…

The accused had confessed she had killed him… but no further words had she said.

Now the expert was called, the oath taken, her case files flagged for the defence,

Permission to quote from them granted, for her task that last day was immense.

In the gallery the reporters lurked smugly, their headlines already planned out…

They wanted a verdict of, *"Guilty,"* for every street vendor to shout.

In the court not one soul thought her innocent… she had killed in a most brutal way,

But the case could not reach its conclusion, till they'd heard what the expert would say.

All eyes were now fixed on the witness, and the woman she'd come to defend,

The prosecutor smiled discreetly, and enquired what new light she could lend?

Witness

"My client was referred by her doctor, as he feared she might take her own life…

"But the woman I met was in desperate need, and criminally abused as a wife.

"Each meeting was fully recorded, and the court possess six of my tapes,

"They are entered as mitigating evidence, and harrowing listening they make."

Narrator

The prosecuting counsel objected, but the judge over-ruled the complaint,

And instructed that the expert continue, which she did without further restraint...

Witness

"My client was clearly in trauma, but my efforts to help her in vain...

"The police service demurred from involvement, and social services did very much the same.

"The first time I met the defendant, she was overcome by tears...

Defendant

"I'm in a dreadful dilemma... and I can't eat or sleep for my fears."

Witness

"Very briefly she nodded a greeting, as I ushered her to a chair.

"Then she seemed to lose her power of speech, so deep was her painful despair.

"She crouched in her shroud of silence, for what seemed a very long while,

"Then recovered herself, with an effort, and grimaced an anguished smile…"

Defendant

"I was young when I met my husband. He seemed kind-hearted, and jolly and bright.

"But my friends warned me to be cautious… He was not what he seemed at first sight.

"I rejected their warnings in anger, accusing them of jealousy and spite…

"We quarrelled, and my dear friends departed… I'd no idea that they would prove to be right.

"My naivety was my undoing, but I trusted that man with my life…

"And believed all his tales of betrayal… even though I was to be his fourth wife!

"He claimed all his wives had been witches, and as mad as lunatic hares!

"They'd abused him… and stolen his money… And I was *the first girl who'd cared!*

"He was clever at plausible stories, as he reeled me into his net…

"Perhaps we believe what we want to? Or I was the most stupid one yet?"

Witness

"I passed her a box of tissues, without comment of any kind,

"And as I watched her nervous reactions, I could see she'd a troubled mind.

"Her face wore perplexing darkness, as she smouldered behind a blank stare…

"She was trembling with a terrible secret, and seemed scarcely to know I was there…

"Each week we met for one hour, but little more was said,

"I knew she was enduring violence and saw injuries to her head.

"The dark glasses she wore served a purpose… like the bandage around her wrist,

"While the purple bruises around her neck, were *not* where she'd been kissed.

"Sometimes, as the recordings testify, she broke into uncontrolled tears,

"But for many weeks she stayed silent, and I learned little more of her fears.

"Until that last morning when I saw her, when her sad eyes looked straight into mine…"

Defendant

"For me there is no future… now I have reached the end-of-the-line."

Witness

"But you're doing fine," I told her. "Please trust me… and say how you feel…

"I haven't come here to judge you… For I know that your suffering is real!

"Suddenly an avalanche erupted, and her grief cascaded like snow...

"Churning her with hysterical weeping... She was prostrate, with nowhere to go.

"I encouraged her to be calmer, and tried to slow the pace...

"Then she collapsed like a worn-out runner, who is weary from a long race."

Narrator

The witness now turned to her papers, while the judge referenced bundles and files...

Witness

"I propose to read from the transcriptions, for the text was carefully compiled.

"You will hear my client speaking, without any prompting of mine...

"For her suffering had lasted for ten long years, before the purported crime."

Narrator

There was shuffling and passing of documents, as the barristers ransacked their notes,

And the jury intently leaned forward... this new evidence might impact their votes.

Defendant

"I came with love to my marriage... but he brought a heart of stone,

"Soon *behind-closed-doors* the abuse began, whenever we were alone…

"To the eyes of the world he was generous… well thought of… A manly bloke!

"But he was, *a Street-God; House-Devil*… Beating me, his idea of a joke!

"Within days I experienced his violence, and his screaming outbursts of rage…

"All the warnings I'd ignored came to haunt me, for now I was trapped in a cage.

"First, he stole my family inheritance… claiming marriage gave him *full legal right*,

"And I was so desperate for his affection, like a coward I put up no fight!

"Once he'd had all my property transferred, on my money his greedy eyes turned,

"Demanding … Where did my millions lie hidden? Then, he started the cigarette burns…"

Witness

"Her voice was a tormented whisper, as though choked by an iron band…

"I waited, and glanced at her briefly, then reached over, and patted her hand.

"She was cold to my touch and unflinching, detached from my curious eyes…

"But her flat and monotonous manner, told me I was not listening to lies.

"I have since checked Land Registry transfers, and *her house was* transferred to his name,

"The man was a vindictive criminal, and this marriage just one part of his game."

Defendant

"Love's story for me was a short one, that fled like mist from my life...

"I found myself married to, Jekyll and Hyde... and not valued at all as a wife.

"How I've yearned for a life that is peaceful, and prayed for release from the strife...

"But his violence grew as the years passed... Many times I have feared for my life.

"That volcano always was bubbling... his rage, the hot coals of my fears.

"If This is LOVE... what is HATRED? I've pondered that question for years.

"He twisted my brain like a corkscrew... wiped mud from his shoes with my hair...

"Battered me daily with insults... and tied me for hours to a chair.

"He screamed I was idle and useless... That I hadn't the brains of a rat...

"Claimed I'm NOT in his league, and surplus to need... That

I'm old and ugly and fat!

"When his adrenalin surge begins rising, hatred's carved in each line of his face...

"I shrivel inside when I look in his eyes, for I know there is no hiding place.

"He has driven away those who loved me, turned my life into one living hell…

"Pushed me right to the edge of madness… I've no family or friends left to tell.

"All that I had, he has taken from me, and abused me worse than a slave…

"Warned me… I will never escape him, until I lie dead in my grave…

"He took my clothes, and burnt them, and threw me into the street…

"Then he forced me to plead, on my hands and knees, when I needed food to eat.

"With HIM I cannot argue… He decides what is right, and what's wrong!

"And he takes kitchen knives to gouge out my eyes, if I'm out of the house for too long.

"He mocks me, and calls me a moron… always bumping and banging around,

"And his mates at the pub say he's married a bitch, when he tells them I'm mentally unsound.

"Last week he left me senseless, when he threw me down the stairs…

"But he laughed, and said… Who'd believe me? No one likes me, and no one cares.

"How can I fight against him? He's too plausible, far too cunning, and strong…

"Whatever he does against me, I will always appear in the wrong.

"How I've yearned to escape the violence, in some place where no anger is heard.

"Or go to sleep and never wake up… or just fly away, like a bird.

"My doctor advised me to leave him… not stay for one moment more…

"But he found the place I was hiding, and beat me… and called me, a whore.

"He bound my wrists, and gagged me, screaming I was out of my mind,

"Then he threw me into a cupboard and padlocked the door behind.

"He laughed to hear me choking, and told me to get used to the smell…

"For I'd seen my last rays of sunlight, and soon I'd be rotting in Hell!

"I struggled all night in bleak darkness, while I fought to break free from my plight,

"And by daybreak I'd sprung the door open! My desperate survival had become a fight!

"When you're locked in a terrible conflict, and you fear that your enemy will win,

"The LAST battle must be for survival… and I knew then I couldn't give in."

Witness

"She opened her bag, and I watched her, as she took out a blood-stained knife...."

Defendant

"This morning, before I came here, I ended his god-damned life!

"I watched the brute lying there snoring, and I pushed this blade into his head...

"Ten years of his vicious hatred are FINISHED... I've killed him... HE'S DEAD."

Witness

"Her words were bleak and hopeless, and came from a broken heart...

"Then she raised the veil across her face, and I saw she was torn apart.

"Her eyes were bruised and swollen... her neck and mouth chaffed raw,

"And her fingers and hands were bleeding, from tearing at her prison door.

"She slumped to the floor in a stupor, still clutching the gory knife...

"And I gently prized it from her, before she used it to end her own life."

Narrator

As the witness's evidence concluded, the courtroom fell silent and dazed,

For the poignancy of those recorded words, left the opposing counsel fazed.

For weeks the case had focused, upon the woman's purported crime,

And dumbly, she'd made no effort to defend herself, during that time.

For years she'd been beaten, and conditioned, into silently accepting blame,

And from the court she'd expected no mercy, only bitter castigation, and shame.

The judge was not swayed by pity, but by revelations of terror and dread.

This new evidence was compelling, concerning the man who was dead.

For a moment he sagely reflected… before the public gallery erupted in noise,

And he was moved to turn his anger, to restoring decorum and poise…

Once the ushers had cleared the court room, he solemnly resumed his place,

There was controlled rage in his bearing, and the power of, *The Law,* on his face.

The Jury was asked to retire, while the case was adjourned overnight…

For he needed time to consider, the malfeasance which had now come to light.

This case must be declared, *a MIS-TRIAL*, for no other verdict could stand…

There had been prejudicial mal practise, with the suppression of evidence, planned.

In his chambers both legal teams gathered, where His Honour demanded to know….

Judge

"Why was the defendant imprisoned, for ten months, during this fiasco?

"I'm appalled by such legal misdirection, and the vital facts never revealed…

"Because she had signed a confession, did you judge that her fate had been sealed?

"You prepared a Brief, of hearsay evidence, while she languished in prison on remand,

"Is this what you purport to be Justice, and conjecture is the

Law of Our Land?

"Marriage is a Legal Institution, where each partner holds Equality of Rights,

"It is not a legalised bondage, where with impunity a man may abuse his wife.

"All acts of violence are criminal… including coercion and

verbal abuse,

"Our laws regard *all* breeches as abhorrent... and marriage permits NO legal excuse.

"Defence Counsel has failed, abysmally, to reveal the circumstances predating the crime,

"And ignored ALL mitigating, WHYs; WHENs; and WHEREFOREs!

You had ten months of preparation time!

"Without the evidence of The Expert Witness, we would never have learned the truth...

"Shamefully you disregarded that, Rule of Justice, which relies heavily on, the Burden of Proof.

"Our Laws value, the Presumption of Innocence, until guilt is unquestionably proved...

"Justice must protect, *the-Defenceless*... it is NOT a variable, for casual abuse.

"Ending any life is MURDER, when *deliberate malice* predicates the crime...

"And Murder is frequently committed, during felonious acts of innumerable kinds...

"But the Case, which was brought here before me, lies outside the range of such acts...

"The defendant showed NO premeditation, which I accept as a now proven fact.

"You brought to trial ... *A VICTIM*... abused and driven half out of her mind,

"By the malicious violence of her psychotic husband…a disgrace to all humankind.

"We are lawyers, and must administer Justice… This is no jungle, where… Might is Right!

"And the evidence speaks of her gentle nature. She was never provoked to a fight.

"The story of her sadistic degradation, will be published in the Public Domain.

"And as representatives of our system of Justice, I hope you sincerely feel shame!

"I find no evidence of … Premeditation… In her torment she did not plan to kill…

"Every living human being has a breaking point, and that morning her blind terror made her ill.

"In these circumstances, I do not find her, GUILTY… for she has suffered terrifying duress and strife,

"What was done came from mind-bending terror, and in defending her own threatened life.

"She has languished for ten months in prison, and in mercy I will not impose more…

"She will leave my court a free woman… with no blot or stain of a crime,

"And may God in Heaven, grant her Mercy, and tranquillity, in the fullness of time."

HOME TO STAY

When schooldays are over, and the big world beckons you,

Maybe you'll pack your bags, and head out into that hopeful blue?

Home is left behind… *a golden future*, beckons ahead…

But never forget where your roots are… or what your mamma said…

> *Chorus* "Home to stay… looking for a bright tomorrow?
>
> There, maybe, roses all will be in flower…
>
> Home fires are always warm and glowing,
>
> Though the skies outside be rain or snowing…
>
> When you are home to stay."

Roads may lead you far… days may all seem grey,

When fortune never comes to help you on your way…

But if you lay your pride aside, and let the cobwebs blow,

Then very soon you'll recognise, the only way to go… is…

Friends may be hard to find… when your luck is down,

But there's a place where smiles grow out of every frown…

Just turn your footsteps back, and throw your pride away…

And hurry back along that well known… well-loved way…

A WINTER'S TALE

There's a harsh north wind blowing, it's stripping the trees,

And the overnight frosts whitened flowers and leaves;

The breath of cold winter breathes hard every night,

And the skies are still dark, in the bleak morning light.

The glories of summer have faded and gone,

And winter has silenced the autumn's last song.

The bare fields lie fallow, turned by the plough,

Where the foraging rooks scavenge hungrily now.

Each day dawns in silence... summer's song birds long flown,

Now Brave Robin redbreast, greets the mornings alone.

In gloom the old year creeps to its close,

And the short days fade quickly, into firelight repose.

But see, in the hedgerows, holly berries glow bright,

And homes gleam, where green fir trees hang garlands of light;

Bleak winter can never suppress Christmas joy,

While its message of happiness fills each girl and boy.

And the angels still herald their sweet story of old,

When their anthem of, Peace, Hope, and Love is retold.

For across the whole Earth, still the Christmas star shines,

As it once shone on Bethlehem, in those long-ago times.

The story is old...but the message fades never...

For Christ is our Saviour, and His Truth lives... forever.

ASPECTS
OF
HUMOUR

THE CHURCH FETE

The vicarage gardens of Saints Peter and Paul,

Were thronged with parishioners and filled with bright stalls.

It was August Bank Holiday, and the annual fete,

With dozens of helpers pouring in through the gate…

Each one wanting to make it a happy event,

With competitions and prizes… and tea served in a tent.

The *WI* had baked cakes, and made strawberry jam,

And the *Friends-of-the-Church* had brought eggs, cheese, and ham.

Mystic Sarah was there, to read tea leaves and palms,

While *The Boys'-Brigade Band,* droned church music and psalms…

They'd intended to play lively music and pop,

And rehearsed every evening, in the back room of a shop.

But the curate insisted, (at the top of his voice),

They must start with, *Abide-With-Me,* and stick to *his* choice.

He'd dismissed *all* they'd practised, and claimed … HE knew best…

They must follow, *his programme*, and forget all the rest!

If they acted rebellious, they'd get nothing for tea,

So, they'd better behave, and play… *Abide-With-Me.*

As a result, the disgruntled young lads were morose,

And the Vicar complained, their efforts couldn't sound worse.

They were murdering the music… But what could he do?

The fete would be opened by, *The Lord Bishop*, at two!

At ten to eleven he went down on his knees

Praying for a miracle to blow in on the breeze.

But no miracle came… only storm clouds instead,

And the poor man grew frantic and quite lost his head.

The marquee was erected at half past the hour,

Followed by a HUGE row… and a heavy rain-shower.

The *Women's Guild* insisted THEY had hired the marquee,

And promptly moved in… and arranged it for tea.

No other group had offered to chip-in for the rent…

So, they set up their tea-urn inside the big tent.

They were doing the catering and providing the food,

And without preparation, tea-time wouldn't look good.

The bolshie, *Young Mothers,* claimed their, *Baby Show*, must prevail…

Then, *the Gardening Club* arrived, with their produce in pails…

They claimed the marquee for their glorious display,

And the judging that followed, at the end of the day.

Pandemonium broke out… while the Vicar couldn't be found…

The violent discord had driven him to hide underground.

He'd gone to find shelter inside of the crypt…

Feeling out-of-control, and his authority stripped!

Suddenly, dozens of chairs were dumped in the marquee,

And the verger fell among them, and gashed open his knee…

The St John's contingent carried him off to their van,

And bandaged him up, like the invisible man!

He continued hobbling around, in the chaos prevailing,

With discordant sounds of *Nearer-My-God-To-Thee,* wailing.

The row in the marquee quickly turned into a fight,

With fisticuffs, and everyone claiming *they* were right!

The *Women's Guild* stoically made sandwiches and tea,

Setting up all the tables where they thought they should be.

At the gate a great gathering of visitors had arrived,

With cages of small animals, for the pet-show inside.

There were rabbits, and guinea pigs, white mice, and rats,

Someone's goat, and a pig, and a variety of cats.

Parrots squawked, the pig grunted, dogs were barking…
and worse…

When a funeral party turned up with a hearse!

They were enquiring directions, and hadn't come to stay…

So, the verger lurched over, and sent them on their way.

Trying to present a calm, Christian Face,

The Choir carried a banner, and marched all-round the space…

It said, "Give generously. Help us restore the church spire,"

But the water smudged words now read, "Give… Hell… or your future is dire."

The *white elephant stall* was piled high with strange things…

Surgical appliances, a wooden leg, and red rubber rings…

One of the toddlers soon got his head stuck inside one,

Then a dog grabbed his coat, and began dragging him along…

The child's mother panicked and started to scream…

And the Vicar was still missing, and nowhere to be seen.

Mystic Sarah left her booth and joined in the fray,

Accidentally upending the *Gardening Club's* appetising display.

Vases of flowers went flying, and many were broken,

Soaking *the Friends of The Church* in the chaotic commotion.

Then the goat escaped, and ate all the scattered prize flowers,

While the pig dined on cheeses, and huge cauliflowers.

The band threw down their instruments, and fought over the cakes…

While the curate lost his cool… and developed the shakes.

The baby-show entrants and their mothers started crying,

As the fete fell apart… with nobody buying!

There was tumult below… and overhead a storm looming,

And those at the gate soon abandoned their queuing.

The dogs, for *the Obedience Test,* ran amok barking,

Fighting over the ham… while *The Bishop* was parking!

With a deep clap of thunder, the heavens deluged rain…

The marquee suddenly, collapsed… and the booths did the same.

Soon the garden was lost beneath inches of mud,

And the fete was awash like a miniature flood.

Beneath his umbrella *The Bishop* gazed at the ruin…

"Oh, dear me," he sighed, "I suspected a storm might be brewing…

Such a wonderful effort… now a devastating picture…

It reminds me of something we read of in scripture!"

The Vicar came hurrying, amid lightning and thunder…

He was wet to the skin… which was really, no wonder.

"My Lord! What calamities we've experienced today…

I apologise humbly, that it's turned out this way!"

The bishop patted his arm, and climbed back in his car.

"Fortunately… unlike old Moses… I haven't come far!

Misfortune overtakes us without rhyme or reason…

Or perhaps it's just something to do with the season.

Whatever it is… God always knows best!

Even bless'd Abraham, was put to the test!

You must rise to the challenges… whatever they may be…

Perhaps there's a message that you're failing to see?

Don't worry… the End-of-the-World hasn't come…

There's always tomorrow, so don't look so glum.

Problems come out of nowhere… like a flash in the dark…

Just remember… Blessed Noah survived forty days in his ark!

The rain that fell on him was much worse than today,

And by morning, these problems will've all gone away."

Then he turned to his driver with a beatific smile…

"There's no need to hurry… my dinner's not yet for a while…

But if I get home by four… there'll be time to have tea!

A pot of Earl Grey… and some fruit cake, for me!"

He waved his hand gaily to the Vicar, (all wet and blue),

"Goodbye, my dear brother… Pax Vobiscum, to you."

THE ALLOTMENT GARDEN

We decided to grow our own veggies…

"Good idea," said the family and friends…

"We'll enjoy peas picked fresh from the garden,

And spinach… broccoli… and carrots… with no bends!"

So, we sent off an Internet Order,

For raised beds, to protect home-grown crops…

And we spent many hours in construction…

With plugs of veggie seeds, sown in small pots.

Such care we took nurturing those seedlings…

Tomatoes, onions, and green peas,

And we dreamed of the strawberries we'd harvest…

And the leafy spinach we'd gather in sheaves.

When all was arranged, the time came for planting,

In our specially built, sturdy raised beds…

And the weather was kind, as we worked happily

On our knees… never raising our heads.

The weeks passed, and all our seedlings flourished,

For we tended, and watered them well…

And we ventilated the greenhouse very carefully,

So the tomatoes grown in bags there would swell.

We gave the peas frames to climb taller,

With the leeks set in small, fertile holes…

While the turnips and potatoes we earthed up,

And the cucumbers were strung up on strong poles…

In June the allotment looked lovely,

Everything we'd sown, was blossoming and green…

What a pride we felt in all our efforts…

And the produce looked fit for the queen.

But July turned into a wet month,

The rain seemed to pour out of a tap…

The tomatoes got black rot, and withered,

And the strawberries were attacked by a cat...

Our allotment adventure was a brief one…

Which caused us nothing but stress…

And in August we faced desolation…

When voracious slugs left us nothing... but a mess!

GROUNDING GRANNY

Granny started flying one Sunday in June…

Her eventual plan was to fly to the moon…

Mr Jones from the Co-op had taught her to fly,

And he'd shown her the tricks of staying up in the sky!

Granddad watched all her antics, and he didn't say much,

When she strutted around looking macho and butch…

She was looping-the-loop, and doing victory-rolls,

As easily as granddad could play carpet-bowls...

While granny was zooming and whizzing around

Granddad much preferred keeping *his* feet on the ground.

She flew under bridges, and over the sea,

And once scared the postman who was having his tea.

She buzzed the church tower, and frightened the bats…

Then skimmed the duck-pond, and was bitten by gnats…

But when she announced... she'd start flying at night,

With the moon as her target… it started a fight.

Granddad shouted… He wasn't having any of that…

So granny made threats… to abscond with the cat…

And refused to be home to make him his tea,

Or rub soothing liniment into his knee…

Their row lead to a deadlock, of… *Who would prevail?*

With granny pushing granddad's head in a pail!

But granddad finally put an end to her tricks…

When he chopped up her broomstick… and made kindling sticks!

IT'S IN THE BLOOD

Uncle Joe was a well-known local gardener

In our village, many distant moons ago…

And he'd filled my auntie's cupboards up with prizes,

For his amazing leeks did well in every show.

As a child I loved to join him in his garden,

Where he gave me little jobs among the trees…

Each week some new adventure lay before me…

Sometimes catching creepy-crawlies, on my knees…

The rewards of uncle's efforts filled our table,

Delicious vegetables and fruit, all cropped and picked…

Potatoes, beans, and sprouts, each in their season…

And in summer, luscious strawberries to be licked…

There was parsley for the fish we ate on Fridays,

And raspberries, for auntie's special home-made jam…

Broad beans, all growing inside their furry jackets…

And green mint, for sauce, to serve with Sunday's lamb.

Uncle's garden was his special private kingdom,

Where he welcomed me as both his niece and friend…

And he taught me many secrets of the garden…

And what it means… to nurture, grow, and tend!

It was there the robin and the thrush both nested,

And there they taught their young ones how to fly…

And many a blackbird sang in the Rowan sweetly,

All summer long, beneath our Northern sky.

Uncle had a way with plants… we'd call… *Green Fingers*!

Whatever seeds he planted always seemed to grow…

And he filled the spaces in between his veggies,

With red roses, and the flower seeds he'd sow.

All year my uncle's garden blazed with colour…

Vivid blooms ran riot in between the shrubs…

'Twixt the beetroot and the spinach there'd be wallflowers…

Tiger lilies, London Pride, and mixed spring bulbs.

My auntie liked to cut flowers for the churchyard,

She carried great bouquets there every week…

To keep alive the memory of her loved ones,

And she'd talk to them… and have a little weep.

Sometimes I went with her to carry water,

While she tidied up… *the great bed*… where they lay…

With their names and dates recorded on neat pillows…

And for each she'd have a message to relay…

But plants were not my uncle's only pleasure…

Joe had ducks and chickens, carefully hatched, and fed…

And a big black pan filled up with tasty goodies,

For their evening meal, before they went to bed.

Each day he boiled this *mash* up for his livestock…

They always knew the time they'd get their meal…

For the clucking and the quacking was quite deafening…

Egg production quite depended on this deal!

By seven o'clock their daily feast was over,

Each little feathered friend, in coop or pen…

The sturdy gates well barred against rogue foxes,

With contented clucking rumbling from each hen.

One evening I recall my uncle saying…

"God gave man hands, so he could hold a spade…

When He opened-up that very first of gardens,

He filled Eden with lovely plants of every shade.

We've been digging holes and growing peas and barley,

Since Adam was munching apples with young Eve!

God put it in our blood, to all be gardeners…

It wasn't a *snake* taught us the way to live!

I'll stick by the golden rule my old dad taught me…

If things don't grow… we'll all just starve and die…

And when I get to heaven… *I want no harp or trumpet!*

Just a place where I can garden… in the sky."

FOOTBALL WITH ALIENS

We went to play football down in the park,

Me and my dad, for a bit of a lark…

We intended to get home to eat lunch at one,

But weird things happened, and the whole day went wrong.

When we got there, at first we'd the place to ourselves…

So we played from eleven, 'til a quarter to twelve.

We were having a great time, and enjoying our game,

Then I messed up a kick, which was really a shame.

The ball didn't go where I'd meant it to be…

It shot up in the air and got stuck in a tree.

There was no way my dad could make it come down…

He threw stones to dislodge it… and called me a clown.

Then he got shirty and said … I'd two useless feet,

And in future I should just play, Hop-Scotch in the street…

We argued, and I said… *Did he think HE was Rooney?*

So he called me cheeky… and a bit of a goony!

Then overhead something shiny appeared in the sky,

It was round like a soup bowl, and hovering high…

"Saints Alive!" Said my dad… "That's a *UFO* up there…

I think we should hide, not just stand here and stare."

We watched horrified as it sent down powerful beams,

Like in weird Sci-Fi movies, or horrible dreams.

Then hedgehogs and squirrels got sucked up in the light...

With their little legs dangling as they vanished from sight!

Then the *UFO* sank silently down on the grass...

It was shining and silver... and *one ginormous mass*!

It had port-hole shaped windows set into its skin...

And strange little faces staring out, from within.

"Good Grief!" hissed my dad... "They're a savage-looking crew...

This could be an invasion coming out of the blue!

If they're sucking up squirrels and hedgehogs to eat...

A couple of humans... will go down a treat!

Your poor mother would never know where we had gone...

And she worries if we stay at the park for too long...

Just think what she'd say if we missed Christmas dinner...

And turned up in May... missing legs... and much thinner!

I don't fancy getting whisked off by that craft...

I've heard Aliens are hostile... so let's take cover fast!"

We ran like scared rabbits, for some holly bushes,

Growing near to a stream... where we hid in the rushes.

Then a small door swished open, and we both held our breath,

As eleven figures popped out... which scared us to death.

We watched, open mouthed, as one sprang up in the tree,

Where our football was stuck... (the one kicked there by me).

He gave it a flick, and it bounced to the ground,

Then his ten little mates started kicking it around.

They were gurgling and making a high squeaky noise,

Like babies all make when they play with new toys…

But as footballers go, they clearly knew none of the rules,

Of the Beautiful Game… and were acting like fools.

So, I took a deep breath… and stood up where they could see…

'cause they didn't seem aggressive, and looked friendly to me.

My dad's face went green, then yellow then red…

But he stayed under cover, with his traffic-light head!

He was crouched in the mud, like a strange neon-light…

Where nobody could see him hiding from sight…

While I walked across boldly, to where they were standing,

Waving my arms about and trying to look brave and commanding!

The aliens stopped playing and formed a straight line,

That reminded me of Wembley before kick-off time.

I wanted to show *how* the game should be played…

And the little men watched, as my skills I displayed.

I dribbled and headed… showing off to their team…

While they quickly caught on and saw what I must mean…

The skills of a league player don't just happen by chance,

That stuff requires *practise* if you hope to advance!

For an hour and a half, while dad hid without speaking,

I coached them, giving football a new Cosmic meaning...

They quickly showed talents I never could have known,

For they took to the game like it was really their own.

They whizzed around showing incredible skill and agility,

And manoeuvred the ball with amazing ability.

The speed they could move, defied our laws of gravity,

And a ref might've considered their skills alien depravity!

But that game was a lesson in *Cosmic Communication*,

And they took to it eagerly, on their little vacation…

Dad stayed quiet as a log, never showing his face…

All muddy and wet and a cowardly disgrace.

He just kept his cell phone dry in his pocket,

While I played football with aliens… all round their space rocket.

When the game was over, I gave them my ball…

And my blue Chelsea strip, which delighted them all.

The squirrels and hedgehogs were safely returned,

With no damage done… and no bridges burned.

Then without understanding what each other might say,

We parted as friends… and they zoomed on their way…

Now I'd like to believe that way out in space,

Football links them to us… and the whole human race.

Once they'd gone, dad cautiously crept out of his cover…

Saying, *"I don't think we should mention any of this to your mother…*

Let's just tell her what happened, was... you lost your ball...

Then got stuck up a tree, and scared stiff you might fall!

We were late home 'cause I struggled for ages getting you down...

It's easier than saying... you've been with aliens, playing the clown..."

I gave him a piercing, **really withering look**...

"Don't call ME, a clown dad... it was you who hid in the brook!

While I taught them, footy... which is the game they now play...

You played hide-and-seek in the mud, keeping out of the way!

I'm not the one spent this afternoon getting muddy...

So, man-up dad, and don't be an old fuddy-duddy!

Just admit it... While you were a coward and stayed hidden away,

***I played, football in the park... with aliens,* today!**

When mum asks... just say, '"*Sorry, dear, we lost all track of time...*

'"*We were having so much fun... in the glorious sunshine.*

'"*And our lad's football skills are so phenomenally clever,*

'"*I felt we should take advantage of this wonderful weather.*"'

"If you take her some flowers, dad, you'll soon be forgiven...

Coming home muddy isn't a crime... and you won't go to prison!"

www.ingramcontent.com/pod-product-compliance
Lightning Source LLC
Chambersburg PA
CBHW071402120626
46546CB00002B/781

* 9 7 8 1 9 6 3 7 1 8 2 2 5 *